THE PARISIAN JAZZ CHRONICLES

THE
PARISIAN
JAZZ
CHRONICLES

AN IMPROVISATIONAL MEMOIR

MIKE ZWERIN

YALE UNIVERSITY PRESS / NEW HAVEN AND LONDON

Published with assistance from the Kingsley Trust Association Publication Fund
established by the Scroll and Key Society of Yale College.

Designed by Mary Valencia

Set in Meridien type by Tseng Information Systems, Inc.

Printed in the United States of America by Vail-Ballou Press

Library of Congress Cataloging-in-Publication Data
Zwerin, Michael.
The Parisian jazz chronicles : an improvisational memoir / by Michael Zwerin.
        p.   cm.
ISBN 0-300-10806-0 (hardcover : alk. paper)
1. Jazz—France—Paris—History and criticism. I. Title.
ML3509.F7Z47 2005
781.65'0944'361—dc22   2005008412

A catalogue record for this book is available from the British Library.

The paper in this book meets the guidelines for permanence and durability of the
Committee on Production Guidelines for Book Longevity of the Council on
Library Resources.

10 9 8 7 6 5 4 3 2 1

To Sam and Kate Hensler and Ben and Martine Zwerin, with love and gratitude.

Many thanks to the discerning and encouraging readers A. Craig Copetas, Sarah Morrow, Howard Mandel, Chris Parker, Chris Erikson, Bill Kirchner, and John Kulka; to Randall Koral for bringing up Johnny Staccato; to my late friends Mel Fishman and Hart Leroy Bibbs; and to point men everywhere.

Swing is the passing of good time.
Calling time don't swing.
Making time don't swing.
Killing time don't swing.
Spare time don't swing.
People with good time got no time to spare.

People called "hip" swing,
*   or they think they do.*
Money don't swing,
*   though what it buys certainly can.*
"Money time" don't swing.
"It don't mean a thing if you ain't got that swing."

Monk swings—the Pope don't.
Russians don't swing.
Generalizations don't swing
*   —it must be possible to find one swinging Russian.*
Black people swing more than white people.
Buppies forget how to swing on purpose.
Black people are funky.
White people who call black people funky don't swing.

Babies are funky (babies swing).
A smile swings.
Farts are funky.

Americans get less funky all the time,
though they can still swing.
The French do not swing,
though they are funky.
Cunnilingus is funky,
but the word don't swing.
If you don't know what I'm talking about—
You probably don't swing.
—Mike Zwerin, recited by Ted Joans on "One O'Clock Jump"
by Zip, on its acid-jazz album *Getting Xperimental Over U*
(Verve/France).

CONTENTS

PREFACE

This book is built around a structure that treats such subjects of my music column in the *International Herald Tribune* as Dexter Gordon, Freddy Heineken, Miles Davis, Bob Dylan, Chet Baker, and Melvin Van Peebles as though they were the written notes in big band arrangements.

Imagine individual parts four or five pages long on the musicians' stands. The written notes are interrupted from time to time with "OPEN" at, say, letters D, M, and T. This means that the instrumentalists should lay out for an improvised solo that will last as long as the soloist has ideas. They wait to be cued back in.

I have overdubbed the book's subjects—all of which were chosen because they had an effect on my life—with "improvisations" consisting of interludes, modulations, tangents, introductions, codas, the running of changes, and shock-cuts leading to images of sex, drugs, and rock 'n' roll. Going from the written to the improvised notes and back again produces an eccentric assortment of realities, fantasies, and fuck-ups in the land of Oobla-dee.

Mike is a misfit, addicted to margins, a dreamer, something of a jerk, innocent in the ways of the world. Although he traveled widely, learned a lot, and had good luck along the way, he was the type of person who always expected worst-case scenarios. He could not find meaning in a life without drugs. Our heartwarming story is about Mike's heroic, uphill, ultimately victorious battle for sobriety and fulfillment.

It's kind of like a screenplay.

Opening credits.

Mike, eighteen, playing trombone with the Miles Davis Birth of the Cool band.

End opening credits.

Mike smoking a joint in the men's room of the executive wing of the offices of his father's Dome Steel Corporation, on romantic Sixth Avenue. He is reading an article about Gerry Mulligan's piano-less quartet with Chet Baker in *Time* magazine. Mulligan was also with the Birth of the Cool. How come Mike is stuck in the fucking steel business?

If music is, as Duke Ellington said, a musician's "mistress," Mike is shamelessly unfaithful to her. He lies to her, cheats on her, abuses her, throws her out in the cold when he doesn't need her anymore. Despite being married to a demanding day gig, he is still in love with his mistress. He hires an executive assistant who was once married to a trumpet player, and who thus understands such things, to help him sneak his horn out of the office for business lunches that are in fact record dates. Business time-outs are also necessary in order to rehearse and record with the Third Stream Orchestra USA. Monday night gigs at Village clubs result in the need to cover his ass for late arrivals at the office on Tuesday mornings. By now he is CEO of Dome Steel. It is grotesque.

Abandoning his family's business and music at the same time, he leaves to become European editor of the *Village Voice,* after which he disappears into the South of France. Mike was good at disappearing. Surfacing in Paris, he writes for the *Trib,* publishes four books, and plays trombone around Europe with ensembles such as the Charles Mingus and George Gruntz big bands, the New York Jazz Repertory Company, and his own groups Not Much Noise and Zip.

The short episodes called Barbershops & Whorehouses are a collection of the hair ends and the come worth saving from the rest of my thousand or so weekly columns, squashed, like most journalism, by deadlines, space limitations, narrowly defined hooks, and self-censorship.

Slow fade.

THE PARISIAN JAZZ CHRONICLES

1

POOP AND HASSE-OLES

THERE IS A GREAT DEMAND JUST NOW FOR THE
ALIENATED AMERICAN.

—HENRY JAMES, *THE PORTRAIT OF A LADY*

Mike and his almost sort-of ex-wife Marie-France were sitting on
the terrace of a café on the Place de la Bastille betting on who
would be the first pedestrian to step in the big pile of dog poop in
the middle of the sidewalk. People kept veering to one side or another, taking instinctive corrective steps at the last second.

Mike called the loser. On the nose—or rather on the sole. The
victim's bowler hat fell off while he mumbled "bloody . . ." in English, and wiped his shoes with his *Financial Times,* which, printed
on salmon-colored newsprint, is perfect for cleaning dog doo.

Like the Lenny Bruce routine about Puerto Ricans and garbage,
the French love dog shit so much they'll steal it from next door
and move it in front of their own house. Or better yet, dump it on
the public sidewalk. Not really, Lenny was joking, but it's the same
joke. Sooner or later somebody—probably some stupid foreigner—
will step in it. Beautiful. *Génial.*

Foreigners wonder how such a highly developed culture can
allow so much dog poop on its sidewalks. The Socialist mayor of

Paris pushed through a law stipulating a 183 euro fine for not cleaning up after your dog. Lots of luck. Mike's theory was that the Algerian who stabbed the mayor one night was not actually, as was thought, a rabid homophobe — Mayor Bertrand Delanoe was gay — but a poopophile. The French consider dog poop on a sidewalk a cultural exception. Delanoe recovered.

Unlike the majority of her compatriots, Mike's almost sort-of ex-wife is user-friendly with non-French names. Marie-France called his smuggler friend Bush "Bulsh" — which fit him totally. A painter named Kanovitz became Cannabis. An Irish cook named Seamus, who hit shamelessly on women, was Shameless. She had exceptional comfort with foreign names, and the English language in general, for a French person. It did, however take years to make her understand that "asshole" is not polite conversational English, or even American.

She was so cute when she said it: "Hasse-ole."

Adding an "h" where there should not be one and subtracting the one that's there is a metaphor for the way Francophiles relate to Anglophiles. The English call a condom a "French letter." The French call syphilis the "English disease." One expression French women use when they start menstruating is: "The English have landed." In general, Euro-neighbors land hard on one another. Italian Prime Minister Silvio Berlusconi told German jokes. Germans tell Polish jokes. The French are famous for joking about foreigners who fail to speak the French language properly. The French mispronounce non-French names on purpose. A non-French name is not to be taken seriously. A name in any other language is not proper.

Mike disliked the way the French pronounced his first name, "Mick-a-yel." The guttural Parigo pronunciation sounded like working-class Arabic — worse, like a French joke about working-class Arabs. At an age when responsible professional journalists tend to go in a more formal direction, adding their middle initial, Michael changed his byline to Mike. The French pronounce it "Mahik," with a nice slow drawl.

When he was younger, Mike's uncle Max had told him—it was sad to hear: "I'm afraid that the working man will have to find another solution to his problems than the labor movement." Uncle Max had been a labor organizer for the left-wing CIO in the steel mills in Alabama in the thirties. He'd put his life on the line. The labor movement was his life. He had a thick head of steel gray hair and an unlined face for his age, but he smiled reluctantly, and his eyes were steely. After being beaten up by company goons, he carried a revolver. When he could no longer avoid seeing that the gangsters were taking control, he joined the federal arbitration agency the National Labor Relations Board as the lesser of two evils. To be more "American," he changed his name to Mike. Uncle Max joked that this was probably the first time in history that an uncle had named himself after a nephew. Later, Michael named himself after the uncle who had named himself after Mike.

The French are not good travelers. "Why leave France?" they ask. "France has everything you need." And, indeed, there are snowy mountains, fertile valleys, an ocean, a sea, surf, beaches, canals, palm trees, lakes, fertile farmland, and thick forests. Unlike in America, what man has constructed in France mostly adds to, not detracts from, the scenery.

Mike and Marie-France took a decade out in the Vaucluse, a spectacular and peaceful valley in southern France running east from Avignon and north of Aix-en-Provence. It had been dubbed "the French California" by the Belgian hippies who, you might say, "discovered" the place. Living there, Mike learned that there was a layer of history, a map of nations, buried but not yet quite dead underneath the map of European states. The "South of France" had been superimposed over an ancient culture called Occitania. There were similar layers in Brittany, Catalonia, Wales, the Basque country, and Lappland. All of them were about some sort of devolution of power.

In the middle of it, Mike got the idea to write a book about it. His pitch was bought by a British publisher run by an English Marxist who disapproved of the title, *Comes the Devolution*. Mike thought it was really neat. But the publisher said: "Devolution is the name the reactionary central authorities use. They think of devoluting power to the people as a gift when in fact it's a basic right." It was eventually published as *A Case for the Balkanization of Practically Everyone*. The publisher went bankrupt. Don't ask.

Researching it, Mike flew up to Kiruna in Swedish Lappland from Marseille, the nearest international airport to the French California. Kiruna was a boomtown in the wild north. Iron, copper, nickel, and chrome had been discovered in quantity. Jackhammers, bulldozers, and climbing cranes were everywhere. Suburban streets spreading into exurbs. German freezers for sale in Swedish Lappland. Volvos everywhere. The only cinema in town showing "Memories Within Miss Aggie," American porn à la Ingmar Bergman—the perfect image for Kiruna.

The book was about "internal colonialism"—modern states superimposed over and exploiting ancient nations. There had been troubadours in Occitania while the French were still living under rocks. Occitan and Catalan, spoken in northeastern Spain, were cousins. Frenchmen who spoke Occitan but not Spanish could have a conversation with Catalonians who didn't speak French. The northern Basque country came to be in southwestern France, and the southern Basque country is in northern Spain. Mike interviewed a former member of the military wing of ETA, the Basque liberation movement, in his small café in St. Jean Pied de Port, in the French Basque Country. He said he had retired from the terrorist organization because it had become too Marxist. "But don't get me wrong," he said. "I'm not anti-Communist, I'm anti-*Spain*."

Similarly, the Lapps were anti-Scandinavian. Sami was the Lappish people's name for themselves. Even their name was occupied by Scandinavians. Young Swedes were coming up to Kiruna to hustle for a few years and take a bundle back south to the capital. It is the type of situation that has been described as "colonial." Mike rented a Beetle from a blond-bearded speed freak whom he had seen jamming gears around town, and in intense conversations in the lobby of the Ferrum Hotel. He drove north to Kautokeino, the capital of Norwegian Lappland. The road was a two-lane asphalt strip through what was called "the last wilderness in Europe." Thirty miles between lonely gas pumps on desolate tundra. In August, the secondary roads were all melted, and many villages could not be reached without a snow scooter or a very long walk. The Finnish border at Kersuando was a bright yellow barge across a rushing blue river. Not much of a border, a loose frontier. Norwegian immigration was a wooden shack next to a drop-pole over the road. Another easy border. But borders nevertheless. Imposed national borders cutting up an ancient nation. To telephone from Kiruna, Swedish Lappland, to Kautokeino, Norwegian Lappland — some three hundred kilometers apart — the connection went fifteen hundred kilometers south to Stockholm, over to Oslo, and back up. The mail went the same way.

Riding back down south to the northern Norwegian city of Trondheim, where there was an airport, Mike was surprised to find himself sharing a train compartment with a couple of French tourists, a man and a woman. French tourists were rare abroad so he paid attention to them. They were both young, slim, tan, and beautiful. He had deep black eyes and a healthy head of curly brown hair that looked as though it would turn gloriously white rather than fall out. He must have been a pianist. In an article in the June 13, 1904, Paris edition of the *New York Herald Tribune*, headlined "Music Affects Hair": "The influence of music, as demonstrated by a series of experiments, was the subject of a remarkable paper read by Mrs. Amelia Holbrook at the Actor's Home, Staten Island, yesterday. Certain kinds of music, asserted Mrs. Holbrook, prevent the hair from falling out, and other kinds produce baldness. Those who play their own compositions on the piano preserve, and often acquire, a luxuriant growth of hair. The violoncello and the harp also have a tendency to preserve the hair, but wind instruments, especially the trombone and the cornet, are fatal to the hirsute adornment." Mike was a trombone player and turning prematurely bald. The French tourist's companion was a redhead and freckled, with minimal makeup, and she had that wonderful misty-eyed, world-weary, show-me-something look French women have. The train went through forests and mountain valleys, it rimmed fjords, and it was daylight until eleven, but the couple looked only in each other's eyes. Like most French people, they talked a lot, with passion, often at the same time. They talked about Luis Buñuel's movies, a new book by Andre Glucksman, about Bob Marley and Jacques Brel, about François Mitterand, about the surfeit of Algerian immigrants, and about their studies. Mostly, they talked about food — about Provençal salad, Alsatian sausages, sauce for the goose, her grandmother's onion soup. She took out a pen and wrote the recipe down for him.

To their credit, the French are human beings like the rest of us. Smile at a French person and chances are you'll get a smile back. Or you won't. Like anywhere else. Finding out he lived in Paris, an Israeli *journaliste* Mike met at an Italian jazz festival asked him: "How can you live with the French? They're so rude. They think they're better than everyone else." Mike reminded her that some people say something similar about the Israelis, and she exclaimed: "Oh. That's different." When Mike was flying into Charles de Gaulle Airport on British Airways on the night French francs were discarded for euros—it was New Year's Eve—a talkative English steward (probably gay, not that there's anything wrong with it) asked him if he didn't mind living with the French. "They're so rude," he said.

Riding into town from the airport, Mike scored a friendly taxi driver. Neither African nor Asian—immigrant drivers are often friendly—this was the devil himself. A white, male, working-class Parisian. The heart of the beast. We all know how rude they can be, right? Probably a right-wing, macho Le Pen voter in addition—the racist cunt. When Mike asked him how he was doing so far with the new currency, the driver answered: "It's no big deal, we'll survive. We French have to learn that we are part of a bigger world. It's probably better for the economy anyway. You have to adjust to change in our day and age." The voice of Euro-sanity. It was a beautiful day. A bright winter sun was up. Driving down Rue de Bagnolet through the peeling twentieth arrondissement to his place in the eleventh, Mike looked out at the human-scale urbanscape and its multiracial assortment of early risers carrying baguettes, and said to nobody in particular: "I really love this town."

Realistically, Paris would probably not be Mike's final resting place. His almost sort-of ex-wife asked him what she should do if . . . She hesitated—he was too old for her. Like Mike, Marie-France tended to dwell on worst-case scenarios. The best Mike could come up with, not nearly good enough, was that she should sprinkle his ashes over the Atlantic. He was an alienated American, a wandering Jew, a musician playing to empty houses on an endless foreign tour. New York would be as absurd a place for him to be buried as Paris. Or Jerusalem, for that matter. Pity he was not a Buddhist —Charles Mingus had his ashes spread over the Ganges. During the seventies, when Mike lived in the French California, he had thought for a minute that maybe the villagers would allow him to be buried in their cozy little cemetery in the *garrigue* up the hill. But that had been thirty years earlier, in the ancient land of Occitania.

So he seemed to be doomed to spend his golden years stuck in a city where he had no roots, in a country with which he had no ancestral connection, and where he had no blood family and no childhood friends. Thirty-five years of exile is no lark. Not even a canary. Isolation was taking his breath away. He'd blown it. It was breathtaking. There were no old buddies to call to help get him through the night—there were no new buddies either. One-dimensional, a blur, a smear, a blip, Mike was ending the song of his life on a held whole note, a capella. He was on permanent loan to Paris, like a painting in a museum.

It has been said that there is only an inch of difference between life in Paris and New York. True enough, but it was the inch he lived in. Notice that after more than thirty years in France, he still thought of it as an inch and not a centimeter. It was no-man's-land by any measure. Everybody had started badmouthing the French. The Europeans were continuing a long tradition. In America there was talk about freedom fries and surrender monkeys. There were jokes: "What happens when you wind up a French doll? It surrenders." A lot of ignorant Middle Americans agreed with Dubya's remark to Tony Blair that the trouble with the French is that they don't even have a word for entrepreneur. That Israeli journalist in Italy had asked Mike if it was bad being Jewish in France now. She'd read about the desecration of synagogues and cemeteries. He said that he'd rather be a Jew in France than black in America, that the French hate Arabs so much there is not much hate left over to direct at Jews. Of course, the Arabs who live in France hate the Jews, but that's another story. Or is it? Americans tend to think that French anti-Americanism implies anti-Semitism. Maybe it does at that. In fact it may be time to get out of Dodge City.

But to go where? Mike was thinking about having his ashes scattered over Amsterdam. That way he could finally settle in that city which he considered the ultimate level of civilization, and he would not even have to learn Dutch. He'd liked living in France better before he learned French. To be alone in public and not to understand what's being said around you is sort of like being stoned. But sooner or later you have to come down, and you wouldn't believe the boring baloney people say to one another in any language.

The French language had been on Mike's back for three decades. He knew it was *sans espoir* when he learned that the noun *bite*, meaning penis, was feminine. If the French like something a lot, they say *pas mal*, not bad. If they only like it a little, they say *pas méchant*, not vicious. Go figure. Anyhow, you cannot speak any language well until you start thinking in it. Mike's job was to think in English—at least he thought it was. His goal, never achieved, was to speak French with Marlon Brando's American accent in *Last Tango in Paris*. When Mike asked a waiter in a café for *un verre d'eau*, a glass of water, the waiter looked at his watch and said, "*Dix heures moins-le-quart*," the time of day. Note the ten minus fifteen rather than nine plus forty-five. Inbred negativity. Another example: *insortable* means a person who is un-take-outable. Dennis Rodman, for example, was *insortable*. In English you say what is, not what is not. In America, you do it and talk about it later. Mike knew that the waiter had understood him. It was a slap in the face of a stupid foreigner who had not taken pains to stretch his mouth properly. It had nothing to do with the language barrier. He had to admire the waiter's sense of theater. The French call such an act "cinema." The French invented cinema, or so they like to tell you. Misunderstanding foreigners on purpose is considered good cinema. They think they are being sophisticated, not condescending. Makes you feel like a fool either way.

There are many gaps between cultures and individuals—language, male and female, old and young, big and small, black and white, rich and poor, north and south, East and West, left and right, city and country. The sense of humor gap may be the most unbridgeable of all.

A French joke:

An attractive lady in the bar of a quiet country auberge calls the bartender over, and begins by caressing his beard. "Are you the manager?" she asks, stroking his cheek. "Actually, no," the man replies. "Can you get him for me? I need to speak to him," she says, running her hand through his beard. "I'm afraid I can't," says the bartender: "Is there anything I can do?" "Yes, there is." She runs a finger across the bartender's lips and pushes it into his mouth: "I need you to give him a message." "What should I tell him?" the bartender asks. "Tell him," she whispers, "that there is no toilet paper, soap, or towels in the ladies room."

Disgusting. *Dégeulasse.* Revolting, right? Yuck.

Now a French Belgian joke:

Digging a thousand meters down, Russian archeologists discover evidence of copper wire that is a thousand years old. They say this means that the Russians already had telephones a thousand years ago. American scientists dig down two thousand meters and find traces of fiber-optic cables. The Americans say this means that Americans had the internet two thousand years ago. The Belgians dig down three thousand meters and find absolutely nothing, and say this proves that Belgians had cell phones three thousand years ago.

Human beings slipping on banana peels, falling down, and, preferably, hurting themselves are hilarious to a French person. Jerry Lewis, remember, is greatly loved in this country. However, the French never really got the hipster humor born from the twentieth-century combination of the English language with the American urban experience. Lenny Bruce, Mort Sahl, Lord Buckley, Richard Pryor, *Doonesbury*, and even *Peanuts* escape them. On the other hand, they understood the blues before most white Americans. And they got the underground comics, instinctively identifying with the minority attitude, even if they did not understand what was written in the bubbles.

Robert Crumb was considered a major artist in this country. The French were proud that the Michelangelo of the underground comics had chosen to live in France. When he bought a house in a village in the South of France it put the village on the map. Crumb got work from French advertising agencies, and his books were published in French. Comic strips were considered an art form in France. What Crumb really liked most, though, was that the French still listened to that good old-time music that was long out of style in the United States.

When he lived in San Francisco, Crumb used to enjoy "sitting on my stoop and watching America decay." He busked on Fisherman's Wharf with a band called the Cheap-Suit Serenaders: "We had a washboard player. People just walked by like we were shrubbery. Sometimes money would come to us after musical-saw solos." In France, he could earn good money playing the same thing for real live paying audiences. He played mandolin and banjo with *Les Primitifs du Futur* (Future Primitives). They recorded in France and toured around Europe. And he could buy recordings of the ethnic music of North Africa, Madagascar, and the Gypsies of Eastern Europe on 78 RPMs in Parisian flea markets.

"Oh boy, am I a crank," he said. "I can't stand the modern world." "Oh boy" was conversational punctuation, like other people say "wow," "gee," or "like." "I'm an old curmudgeon. Oh boy. Why is it the only music I like was made before I was born? It's torture. I'll be in some train station and there will be this blast of horrible rock music. It's getting harder to avoid. And modern jazz completely bewilders me. I'm in the twilight zone."

Ornette Coleman once said that he could not understand how somebody like a nuclear physicist would want to listen to old-time music. He thought that an advanced thinker should be interested in advanced music. It doesn't work that way. One modern warfare expert—a retired general—tinkered with old Volvos. A gangsta-rap producer collected Renaissance art. Woody Allen, a maker of films, an advanced medium, played dixieland clarinet.

Crumb was happy to be able to report good news for a change: "The accordion is coming back. The new accordion teacher in our village already has ten students. Including me. People butchered the accordion in the fifties and sixties. Everybody played so corny. If you told a girl on a date you played accordion you'd go home alone for sure. After World War II, the accordion went to hell—like everything else. You used to be able to hear a farm woman from Appalachia or the Auvergne sing a folk song. But people just making music because they love to, not to become famous—the opposite end of the spectrum from Madonna—have just about vanished. Now you just push buttons to make music. Everything is prepackaged. You don't have to carry a melody anymore. You just carry a Discman. People used to get together and sing after dinner because it made them happy. That old-time, homemade, frontporch kind of stuff. Making music is just another healthy part of our environment they have taken away from us. Glee clubs, for instance. Remember glee clubs?"

Barbershops & Whorehouses |

After waiting over an hour while journalists with previous appointments filed in and out interviewing Stevie Wonder, Mike's turn finally came. Pissed-off but not disrespectful, he set up his tape machine and said: "It's like a barbershop in here."

Not missing a beat, Wonder jerked his head around and replied: "Or a whorehouse."

2

DEXTER GORDON
LIFE AND DEATH IN THE MARGIN

I LAUGH, AND MY LAUGHTER IS NOT WITHIN ME.
I BURN, AND THE BURNING IS NOT SEEN OUTSIDE.
—NICCOLÒ MACHIAVELLI

A letter from the Romanian Jazz Federation arrived out of the blue one fine morning not long after the fall of the Berlin Wall. President Johnny Raducanu, whom Mike had never met, was asking for advice to help build a jazz scene in his country, which, he said, with some restraint, "had not been possible under the Communist terror."

In the process of answering him, Mike heard on the radio that Dexter Gordon had died in New York around midnight the night before. He did not know whether Dexter had ever played in Romania, but his death would certainly be a sad event in Raducanu's life as well as his own. Raducanu had ended his letter: "Jazz represents a great family without any frontiers."

Although there are many fights within the family, it can still be called familial. Bertrand Tavernier joined the family when he directed a movie starring Dexter Gordon called *Round Midnight*. Mike had played a bit part as a journalist that was left on the cutting room floor. After Dexter died, he called Tavernier for a statement for his column in the *International Herald Tribune.*

"Dexter embodied the tenor saxophone," Tavernier said. The director had been listening to Dexter's classic recording of "Guess I'll Hang My Tears Out To Dry" when Mike called. "He had a voice of his own. He was so intelligent. He had such a sense of humor. I'll miss him very much. Once Dexter entered your life, he never left. He was so civilized. He hated the cliché image of the untutored cotton-picker of a jazz musician."

An untutored reporter was once taken aback when Gordon named Ravel as one of his favorite musicians. "Why are you surprised?" Dexter said, pulling up all of his dignity. "I also like Duke Ellington. Maybe you don't know who Duke Ellington is."

Long-Tall Dexter Gordon was a big man with a big sound who maximized a relatively small musical territory. It was a modest stake, but he was good at fertilizing what he had. In his last years, however, things were no longer so rosy. As he grew older, he became more knowledgeable, and a more interesting—and richer—person. But his musical muse was leaving him. His late improvisations could remind you of baby talk. He relied increasingly on strings of quotations from such songs as "Strangers in Paradise." He became sentimental and syrupy as the irony went out of him. Some people called it innocence. Either way, massive partying had caught up with him. A young drummer who worked with Dexter toward the end called the experience "a crash course in playing slow."

Thelonious Monk once said: "I'm tired of trying to convince them." Dexter had arrived in a similar place. There were good reasons for slowing down. He had kidney problems and diabetes and cancer of the larynx. There were also bad reasons. His cognac consumption, for one, was famed. Fortunately, the fading of his musical vigor coincided with an unexpected late incarnation as a movie star.

Tavernier had had trouble contacting Dexter at first because Long-Tall had not paid his telephone bill. "He was very weak when I first talked to him," Tavernier said. "Weak and skeptical. I am content because I think the role gave Dexter a reason to live."

For playing Dale Turner, basically himself, in *Round Midnight*, Dexter was nominated for an Academy Award. The French Minister of Culture named him a *Chevalier de l'Ordre des Arts et des Lettres* —a Knight of Arts and Letters. When a reporter asked him if he'd like to do another movie, he replied: "Yes, but something easier." He strolled for a minute. "Something lighter. How about *Hamlet*?" Marlon Brando told him that his performance in *Round Midnight* was the first time in ten years that he had learned something about film acting.

Dexter got this idea that he wanted to play an apostle in *The Last Temptation of Christ*. He called Martin Scorsese and said: "Lady Martin"—he called everybody "Lady," like Lester Young—"don't you think a black apostle is a good idea?" "After dying onscreen for about two hours in *Round Midnight*," Tavernier said, "Dexter made a commercial for a life insurance company in Japan. He had a good laugh about that one."

John Vinocur, the managing editor of the *International Herald Tribune,* called Mike with breaking news. Dexter—Vinocur called him Dexter; everybody did—had been detained by customs officers at Charles de Gaulle Airport early that morning. He was out on bail, and if Mike could find him and write something quickly, Vinocur would put it on the front page. It would be historic. Never before had a mass-circulation English-language daily newspaper considered Dexter Gordon front-page news.

John Vinocur believed that jazz was as basic to American culture as the Western movie, and that the *Trib,* an American paper representing the United States in Paris and overseas in general, had an obligation to cover it. Mike had first met him over the telephone from Bonn, where Vinocur was then living while covering Germany for the *New York Times*. Mike and his family were penthouse-sitting in Montparnasse. The penthouse had a landscaped terrace with plants, small trees, flowers, and a fountain. They could see the dome of the Hotel des Invalides in the distance. It was August in Paris. The perfect city—Paris without the French—and it felt like a Hampton. At the time, the late seventies, Mike's stuff was still running only once a month in the *Trib*. Being reachable did not seem essential. He had not left the penthouse's number with the office. Tracking him down must not have been easy.

Vinocur introduced himself over the phone, and asked questions about Chet Baker, whose career was having a surprising late spurt in Europe. In America, the trumpeter was more or less forgotten. Vinocur asked Mike if Chet lived over here now, was he still taking drugs, did he have a European manager and record company, and so on. Mike told him what he knew, and asked why he was asking.

"It's just that I heard him last night in Bonn," Vinocur said. "And I've rarely been so moved by music." Not too many people in positions of journalistic power are moved by jazz music, so Vinocur's eventual appointment as managing editor of *the International Herald Tribune* was good news.

Both before and after Vinocur, newly appointed managing editors inherited Mike uneasily at best. They never quite knew what to do with him. Considering his area of expertise marginal, they questioned his allotted weekly slot. Once they realized that he came with the furniture, the resulting unspoken deal was that they'd continue to underpay him in return for publishing his irrelevant column. Not on staff, he was in a place referred to as a "gray area." He had social and medical benefits and got a monthly pay slip, but it was not a salary. If he didn't write he didn't get paid. Being in a gray area was something like being in the margin. The margin was not such a bad place to be. Marginals have a better chance of staying out of the way of those who run things in this world. Mike was the kind of person who would not join a line waiting for something he thought he needed because the line itself implied that he didn't.

The *Trib* was co-owned by the *Washington Post* and the *New York Times.* The partners took turns nominating the *Trib*'s managing editors. After a shuffle of nine of them, Mike felt a bit like Fidel Castro surviving all those American presidents. Over the years, under the radar, his territory expanded and came to include blues, folk, funk, rock, and world music. Astor Piazzolla was in his territory; Igor Stravinsky was not. He defined his mandate as covering "every kind of music except 'serious' music."

Mike had gone between playing music and writing about it over such a long period of time and with such a consistently wide assortment of substantial tangential interludes that he appeared to be dedicating himself to being marginal everywhere. The rationalization was that dividing his life between making music and writing words was an ecological combination rather than lack of dedication to either one. One he did alone, the other with others. Yin and yang. In fact, he was being unfaithful to two mistresses at the same time. But he considered that he was giving life the good try, and that being shot down would be a testimonial to having been airborne in the first place. Having read Henry James's *The Beast in the Jungle,* he knew that there was no danger of flack if you never took off.

In big bands, the pressure of the melody lines and the responsibility for the section cancelled out whatever prestige came with playing lead trombone. He had no ambition to lead anybody or anything, and he did not have enough air to blow into a bass trombone. Second trombone was perfect. There was the thrill of making music—sitting in the middle of all those fat chords, where only the musicians sitting near him, and occasionally the leader, knew how good or bad he was. Second trombone players, like freelance journalists, generally work so cheaply that if you are any good at all it's not worth the bother for the boss to fire you. Margins must always be staffed somehow.

John Vinocur, on the other hand, was a person who would always be sure to get into the body of the work. No footnote he. He spoke fluent German and French and was at home in the corridors of power. Vinocur was a motivated corporate man who *insisted* on playing lead. He was made managing editor of the *International Herald Tribune* as sort of a consolation prize after coming out on the losing side of a boardroom battle at the *New York Times*, where he had briefly been under consideration for a top editorial job. It was said that he had been too cocky, and that his profile had been too high for his own good. But he knew how to land on his feet. He was sent over to edit the *Trib*, a job for which, he said, he had been born and that he would like to do for the rest of his life. But when, after some years, the *Washington Post* insisted it was time for one of their people to run things, Vinocur got shot down a second time. After which he wrote features for the paper while continuing to be paid his six-figure managing editor salary as per his apparently unbreakable contract. Vinocur knew the importance of written contracts, something Mike had never grasped. Vinocur was a winner. It didn't really matter at what. He was a winner at winning—a professional professional, an authoritative authority. As managing editor, foreign policy expert and syndicated columnist, Vinocur circled the globe on a generous expense account interviewing powerful people. Dressed in ever so carefully rumpled suits, he was the American journalist du jour on French TV. He was on speaking terms with Clint Eastwood. "Clint reads you," he told Mike. He told Mike that the president of the Deutsche Bank liked his stuff. Such compliments to freelancers are generally a no-no in big-time journalism. The "professional" attitude being: "If we print you that's the only compliment you need, and don't even think about asking for a raise." Which is a fancy way of saying spread your legs and shut up. Vinocur encouraged Mike to write about obscure but worthy jazz musicians. They went to the jazz clubs together, they talked about musicians they liked over lunch. It should have been obvious that anybody so high up in the corporate echelons who liked a marginal jazz expert like Mike would inevitably be shot down. A managing editor who liked Mike was by definition not true managing editor material.

Love may be cheap in the world of big-time journalism, but it's not free. Vinocur tracked Mike down still again, in a recording studio near the Bois de Boulogne. He knew that Mike's priority was to play music rather than, or at least as much as, write about it. It was no secret. They'd talked about it. It was one reason he liked Mike. A freelancer, free, Mike had every right to play as well as write about music. When Vinocur was trying to reach him, Mike was recording an acid-jazz album called *Gettin' Xperimental Over You.* Sampled rock beats and other overdubs were added to tunes like Count Basie's "One O'Clock Jump." Acid jazz seemed like a good idea at the time. The album came and went quickly. But while it was being recorded there had been fond hopes. First, the engineer said the red light was on, and would Vinocur please call back. He called back in the middle of a take of Mike's impression of Tommy Dorsey's version of "Getting Sentimental Over You"—not easy to play on a trombone. Mike picked up, and Vinocur said that a major Beatles reissue would be on the market tomorrow, that the EMI Records publicity machine was all cranked up, and that if he would come in right now and write a review, it would run on the front page. Mike explained that he was in a recording studio on a tight budget, that it was his dime, and that the meter was ticking. Vinocur decided not to understand—he wasn't even listening. There was no reaching out. It was clear that there would be no "no" taken for an answer. Sensitivity was not Vinocur's strong suit. This was, after all, the *Beatles*. Vinocur wanted Mike in the office *now*. "You have to get your priorities straight," he said. He could get scary.

Not that there's anything wrong with the Beatles—on the contrary. But choice is what living in the margin is all about. A freelancer is paid less than a staff writer, and in return he does not have to write about something if he doesn't want to. Vinocur had no right to order him into the office. It was, however, clear that a refusal would not be good for Mike's career. Thinking "blackmail," he packed up his horn and ran out of the studio. Taxis were not easy to find in the early evening near the Bois, and it was an hour before he got to the *Trib*'s office in Neuilly. There was not all that much more time than the length of the CD itself to listen to it, decide what to say, and write five hundred words with his usual insight and humor plus front-page panache.

But when Vinocur ordered him to locate Dexter Gordon after his bust at Charles de Gaulle Airport, Mike hit the ground running with verve and impulse! Family is family. A call to a fellow drug fan did the trick.

Long-Tall Dexter was an imposing (six-foot-five) personage—a born star. This was his first French tour since his Oscar nomination for *Round Midnight*. Having become what might be called a big name in a small household, he was wearing his Dale Turner hat from the movie when the customs man said the computer showed that he was still wanted for a twenty-year-old misdemeanor. Arriving passengers recognized Dexter and said hello to him while he and his wife and manager Maxine waited on a bench to be questioned.

A few nights before flying over from New York, he had played a concerto for saxophone, a prestigious affair, in Avery Fisher Hall. Dexter was flying first class these days. He said that he'd never thought a saxophone player could make so much money. But now that the plot was thickening, he spread his hands wide and said: "Remember that guy in *Les Misérables?* I feel like him. They chased Jean Valjean for twenty years for a loaf of bread." His survivor's twinkle and slowly rolling hand movements added twists of irony to his husky voice telling his tale of woe. Dexter had lived the expatriate Saint-Germain-des-Pres lifestyle that *Round Midnight* helped make a pop-culture myth—the alienated African American whose music was ignored at home scraping by on respect and romance in Paris. The jazz caves had been romantically dark and smoky, and the cafés, restaurants, hotels, and French-Connection heroin were cheap. He had been a junkie. It was illegal. He accepted that: "They had observed me buying and I was obviously a user. But it was only possession. I wasn't hurting anyone but myself." The two-month jail sentence he served was "just as well because I cleaned up." After he got out, he had to sign in at the *préfecture* once a week. What with the nature of the French bureaucracy, it took a good part of the morning. He read Henry Miller's *Quiet Days in Clichy* in the *préfecture*.

With his arts and letters knighthood, his Academy Award nomination, and with the help of *Round Midnight*'s producer, Irwin Winkler, Dexter had, despite his earlier arrest, obtained a letter with a three-year visa from French consular officials in New York. When he pulled it out in Charles de Gaulle, the customs chief said: "This doesn't mean anything. The consular people in New York don't know what they're doing." That's a quote: "Le Chef did not want to know anything about any old letter."

Dexter was led into a series of rooms—"you know, like the police do, so your lawyer can't get to you"—while Maxine telephoned for help. "I went nuts on them," she recalled. "I said they were a bunch of fascists and we were going home on the next plane and we'll never play in France again." A sympathetic officer later told Dexter that they would have let him go sooner if his wife had not been so rude: "The officer told me: 'The chef, he's a racist, and he hates Americans. He'll keep you as long as he can.'" On hold in their locker room, Gordon watched cops "keep coming in and digging into their beer stash." With disarming innocence, he said: "Not one of them offered me a taste." He lost his temper only once. When an officer picked up his hat—Dale Turner's hat—Dexter growled: "*Touche pas le chapeau"*—don't touch the hat.

With a slow wink, Dexter said: "I think it's pretty weird that Klaus Barbie benefits from a twenty-year statute of limitations and not me."

In the end, the chief issued a nine-day visa that covered the current French tour, which included a concert for five thousand people in La Grande Halle de la Villette. Before the concert began, Jack Lang, who, as Minister of Culture, had awarded him his *Chevalier des Arts et des Lettres,* visited the dressing room and said: "Dexter, this has been a terrible mistake. Please don't blame the French people for this."

Dexter thought about "all the people this sort of thing happens to every day and you never hear about it. Next time I come to France, I'm going to wear my Chevalier medal." He wanted to take a vacation in Biarritz next time.

Too bad he was not around to laugh at the irony of his dying round midnight.

Barbershops & Whorehouses   II

The things you hear me say today, you're going to hear me take them all back.
—*Ornette Coleman*
I can talk the wheels off a Volkswagen.
—*Waylon Jennings*

3

PLANELAND
BRINGING UP BABY

BIOGRAPHIES ARE WRITTEN TO COVER UP THE SPEED
WITH WHICH WE GO.
—KENNETH KOCH

Planeland—Logan Airport, Boston. This is a message in a bottle
thrown out from an overheated, landlocked, smoke-free island
with a dubious past, no future, and not much of a present.

There is no year in Planeland; no month, week or day—only
endless hours. Neither at sea nor on land and certainly not in the
sky, the sovereign state of Planeland suspends normal dimensions
of time and space. It is late New Year's Day eve. Mike and his
half-French teenage son Marcel are in transit on their way back
to Charles de Gaulle from LAX airport, which is in the American
California. Having spent two weeks auditioning music conservato-
ries in Boston, Miami, and Los Angeles, they'd taken off with three
hours' sleep after Lisa Maxwell's New Year's Eve party on Fairfax
in Hollywood. Maxwell had just finished a tour playing saxophone
with Guns N' Roses. She had a saxophone tattooed on her pelvis
—she showed it to them. Their connecting flight back to Paris is
three hours late out of Minneapolis. Marcel fingers Charlie Parker's

"Blues for Alice" on an unplugged bass guitar in a deserted gate lounge. God bless Leo Fender.

Marcel was born in the city of Nîmes in September 1975—one month before his mother's thirtieth birthday. Marie-France had warned Mike that she'd made up her mind to have a baby before she was thirty. If not with him, too bad; with someone else then. It was a joke more than a threat. At worst, it was a nag. She was a tender, intelligent, beautiful woman but, she couldn't help being French. The French are not like you and me. He had fallen in love with her at first sight, and she'd told him that he was the first man with whom she'd ever had an orgasm (if not with him, with someone else then).

Marie-France barely made her birth deadline in their paradise in the South of France. The *hameau* (hamlet) in which they lived was called Les Grands Cléments, not far from, naturally, Les Petits Cléments. There were no telephones in the hamlet when they moved in. Telephones in France were still a luxury, and when there was a mail strike for six weeks, it was like being washed up on a desert island. They were renting their seven-room house for fifty dollars a month. There were holes in the roof, plumbing was primitive, the heating system was creaky and required continuous attention, the house leaned here and there, it needed plaster and paint, and the septic tank stank. But it was, in its funky way, more of a home than Mike had ever had. Once a month during Marie-France's pregnancy, the mailman rode up on his motor scooter and delivered a three-hundred-franc pregnancy subsidy from the French government. Then President Giscard d'Estaing pushed through a crash national telephone-wiring project. The entire country was connected in one swoop. The hamlet swarmed with workers for a week. Along with the birth of Marcel about the same time, the big phone installation was about the only event that might be called major during their years in the French California. Culturally, it was more like the French Sahara.

One hot afternoon, looking for a way to counter the tedium, Mike decided to celebrate both American and French independence days with an early July day trip. Driving their Volkswagen minibus southward, he passed through the market town Apt, the regional capitol, where Belgian hippies sold dope next to the flower shop, and over the Luberon Mountains to the village of Lourmarin. He could see the Luberon range from his office in the *grenier* on their third floor, a room so big they played ping-pong in it. A spectacular view is not a good idea for the office of a writer. Albert Camus, one of his earliest heroes—Mike felt like a stranger everywhere—had lived in Lourmarin, and was buried there. He died when his sports car crashed during a drive from Lourmarin to Paris. Mike found CAMUS on a headstone in the small, otherwise anonymous cemetery in the *garrigue* next to the village, where thyme and lavender grew wild. It was very hot. Mike was the only living soul around, and he was greatly moved. He wanted to leave a memento for Albert, but he was wearing only shorts and a T-shirt and there was nothing to offer. Remembering photographs of Camus with an unfiltered Gitane hanging from his mouth, he took out a cigarette, tore off the filter, lit it, planted it in the earth near the grave, and stood next to it in tribute for a few moments before driving back home.

Where nothing much continued to happen. Marcel discovered a bat family in the shade behind a stuck shutter. Mike grew a successful marijuana crop in the back garden. One night after midnight, a Belgian hippie named MacDonald woke him up and offered him a sniffette. It was more of a paragraph than a line. The French Connection, then flourishing eighty klicks away in Marseille, hinted at a more sinister definition of paradise.

Later, much later, Mike and Marie-France, by then his almost sort-of ex-wife, returned from Paris to the French California for the funeral of her best girlfriend, Brigitte, who had died down there of cancer. Still legally married, they were living a ten-minute walk apart, not far from the Bastille. Marie-France heartily endorsed such an arrangement. Mike considerably less so. His idea had been to age as buddies together and now they were sort of almost sort-of ex-buddies. Brigitte, who was French, was being buried in the little cemetery, where Mike could never be, above Les Grand Cléments. It was odd, after some twenty years, being back in the same idyllic Provençal countryside he had shared with Marie-France when she still loved him. It turned out that there were more visiting mourners than accommodations for them and so it came to pass that Mike and Marie-France slept together in an icy bed in a freezing room of an unheated farm house opened at the last minute for the occasion in the middle of a cold winter. You'd think the need for warmth, a touch of nostalgia, or just plain curiosity would have pushed them together, but there was neither touch nor cuddle. Afterwards he asked her about it, and she reminded him that it had been her best friend's funeral, for Chrissake, and in any case she always slept poorly. It was true—she would often awaken with a start at the drop of a hat. Mike had never quite taken her complaints about sleeping poorly seriously. He had considered them nags. Looking back, insisting on cuddles had been insensitive of him. Apparently she had slept poorly all of the years they slept together.

Marie-France had learned to have confidence in her own discriminations. She was now a video producer and she was good at it. She liked to joke, but not really, that thanks to Mike she had trouble relating to men who could not tell the difference between Sonny Rollins and John Coltrane.

Mike had been blindsided by her. He thought he had perfected a cutting-edge Jewish American Princess detector. No JAPs on Michael. NAPs are French JAPs. NAP stands for Neuilly, Auteil, and

Passy, three wealthy Parisian neighborhoods in the sixteenth arrondissement where many French Jewesses are raised. He was totally unaware of them, and unprepared for Marie-France.

Driving down to the Vaucluse from Paris, after exiting the Autoroute du Sud at Avignon, they would turn east in the direction of the Bases Alpes, and after half an hour or so there was a bend in the two-lane road on a rise behind the stony hilltop village of Gordes, where they pulled over to admire Roussillon, Minerbes, Lacoste, and the other fairy-tale hilltop villages rising out of the valley below. It was a relief every time. Fewer people were living in the Vaucluse now than in the eighteenth century. There would come a time when Mike and Marie-France would wonder why they had all left.

Barefoot toddler Marcel would knock on the doors of Grand Clementians who would not even say *bonjour* to his "hippie" parents, a.k.a. *les étrangers*. A Parisian was as much of a foreigner as an American in the French California. However the locals loved children almost as much as dogs, and Marcel would always come away with a pat on the head and a goodie.

When the growing lad continued to suck on a pacifier, Marie-France said: "You're too old for that." And said and said. She was right, but a nag's a nag. This went on for four months until, without warning, one fine day (actually, they were all fine in the French California), driving to the Saturday market in Apt, passing some red hills known as the Colorado, Marcel opened the window and tossed his pacifier out at forty kilometers an hour and that was the end of that. The French NAP's nags were sometimes useful.

Marcel's first glimpse at the power of bilinguality came in a camping ground near gently named Tralee, on the western coast of Ireland. The family was spending quality time touring the Republic in their Volkswagen minibus. A bunch of British and French kids were playing pickup soccer as the sun set over the ocean. Having been rejected by them as too little, Marcel was looking on, feeling left out. The players were not communicating; there were arguments, and when they discovered that Marcel could understand both languages, he became the center of attention. Towering over him, the big boys hung on his every word.

A few months later, the Empire State Building was towering over the view just outside the window of Mike's mother's apartment on Thirty-fourth Street and Park Avenue. It was good to be at the center of the world again. The Village Vanguard and the Russian Tea Room were within walking distance. It was also good to have return tickets. New York is a good place to visit but you wouldn't want to live there.

The dollar had gone down to a new low of four French francs. (Remember French francs?) They were living next to a ruin with *1692* carved in stone above the entrance, thanks to a small dollar inheritance, and four-franc dollars were not enough to live on. Their fifty dollars a month rent had in fact doubled. Mike had removed himself from the game. By this time he could not get published on toilet paper or play with a rubber band. For lack of anything else to do, he began to practice the trombone again. He made a record called *Flash* in a local studio with the tiny, fifteen-year-old Michel Petrucciani, a pianist of Corsican ancestry who lived nearby in Montelimar. *Flash* came and went quickly. Mike was running out of options. This visit to New York was in part to look into the possibility of moving back.

When they arrived, Marcel had a highly accented English vocabulary of maybe a hundred words. Glued to Mike's mother's color television screen, he watched Mr. Rogers, *Sesame Street*, cartoon after cartoon, sitcom after sitcom, movie after movie—*I Love Lucy, Dallas, Batman. King Kong.* He took his meals in front of the tube, and got up only to go to the bathroom or to sleep. When it was time to fly back to Paris, washing the dishes, Mike said to Marcel: "Hey, man, you're old enough now. Come over and help me here." Marcel took his eyes off the screen for once, and they were flashing as he said, in a flawless New York accent: "No way." He was six years old.

They moved from the Big Clements to Paris when the father of the NAP offered them the use of a six-flight walkup he owned on Rue Ruhmkorff, overlooking leafy Villa des Ternes in the seventeenth arrondissement. Watching the movie of Jules Verne's *Journey to the Center of the Earth* up there, Mike heard James Mason explain that the reason they could make their historic journey now was because they had their new Ruhmkorff lights. The street had been named after the inventor of the hand-generated electric lights that replaced candles on miner's caps. Old Europe was wonderful.

Mike was a fifty-year-old freelance writer married to an unemployable—she was sure of it at the time—wife, and they had a young son and no savings. Then the dollar began to climb back from four francs, eventually reaching ten. Living between two cultures, you have to be a CFO just to figure out where to buy a shirt. Ten French francs for a dollar was a good deal, and when thirty thousand dollars' worth of his inheritance matured, it was enough for a down payment on an apartment.

Inevitably, the dollar began to go south again. Whatever happened to the gold standard? The trouble with trying to drop through cracks between systems was that you risked getting stuck in the murky land of reciprocal tax treaties and movable exchange rates. The dollar was back down to eight-fifty when a panicky Mike jumped at one of the first apartments he looked at. It was ninety-five square meters on a ground floor not far behind the Bastille in the inexpensive eleventh arrondissement, which, since the opening of the Bastille Opera House, was slowly gentrifying.

Marie-France said that Mike had panicked. Why had he bought

the first apartment he'd seen without consulting her? He said he had so consulted her. She said she did not want to live on the ground floor, and she'd never agreed to live in the still working-class eleventh. Marie-France was smart, sensitive, a loving mother and a good lover, but she was also insecure and she resisted change with great dedication. She was, after all, a NAP. Mike preferred to think of it as an incisive decision made with great courage in the nick of time for the good of the family. It was, however, also true that he was a person who was always early to appointments. He answered questions too quickly, without enough reflection. He was afraid of his own silences. He liked writing for a daily paper because his pieces were published almost immediately; he was hooked on instant gratification. He took aspirin *before* he got the headache.

They qualified for a fifteen-year mortgage thanks to a shifty, blond, blue-eyed hustler with a moustache and a twitch in a three-piece pinstripe suit. They called him Monsieur Goye. M. Goye, an officer in the Paris branch of the Loan Potato bank, had volunteered his financial services gratis because, Mike was sure, he was stuck on Marie-France's sister Mathilde. Mathilde had been a member of the Claudettes, six half-naked beauties wearing bondage chains dancing on stage and screen behind the late variety star Claude ("My Way") François. Looking back, Goye must have raked something off somewhere along the line. At 13 percent interest, there was some room for raking-off. The walls were thin, the elevator machinery was right under their bedroom, there were leaks and unexpected expenses, and Marie-France slept more poorly than ever. Basically, the ground floor apartment in the eleventh arrondissement marked the end of their love affair.

Mike read Asterix in French, and Garfield in English, to Marcel at bedtime. They'd break up at Obelix hauling his stupid *menhirs* around; laugh at the character named Assurancetourix (all-risk insurance). They'd giggle at Garfield suffering a nap attack. There was an American book about a lazy duck whose operative line—"I'm taking it easy today. I'll do it tomorrow"—they adopted as a motto. They played squash on a court next to the JAPY gymnasium, where Jews had been put on trucks for Germany during World War II. Marcel won all the time, the little shit. No, that's not nice. Mike did not want to think like that. Strike it. It's just that the kid kept hitting winners in corners and he wasn't even aiming. He'd hit similar spooky winners from impossible angles on a tennis court. Mike would get furious when Marcel beat him at backgammon. Then he'd get furious with himself. Who was the grownup here? Watching the Davis Cup final France won against the U.S. in Lyon in 1991 on television, they were surprised to find themselves rooting for the French. For that one weekend, Henri Leconte was the best tennis player in the world. It was a spooky state of grace. His winners reminded Mike of Marcel's, and the puzzled look on the face of the defeated young Pete Sampras was, he imagined, similar to his own.

Thanks to some good bureaucratic moves by Marie-France, Marcel was able to attend the Victor Hugo junior high school around the corner from the Picasso Museum in the Marais. It's called a *collège* here. King Henri IV set up his court in the Marais in 1609. The finest architects and stonemasons in Europe built townhouses and *hôtels particuliers* for the nobility. In the 1680s, Louis XIV moved the court to Versailles, and the neighborhood fell into disrepair. Brothels multiplied on the narrow, garbage-strewn streets. It was for centuries a neighborhood zoned for small industries— warehouses, craftsmen, artists. In 1962, de Gaulle's Minister of Culture, Andre Malraux, subsidized wide-scale renovation. Buildings were restored rather than demolished. Old ceiling beams were stripped of plaster and oiled. The entire quarter got a coat of paint. As rent control phased out, rich Americans and Arabs moved in.

The boulangerie where Marcel and his friends bought *pain au chocolat* for their afternoon snack was a classified historical monument. He walked to and from school—it wasn't all that far—in the splendid architecture of that living museum as if he owned it. The route took him through Place des Vosges, a seventeenth-century square with a garden surrounded by arcaded buildings from the time of Henri IV. There was a parking garage under it by then, and a new playground had been installed, but it remained a sought-after address. Victor Hugo lived on Place des Vosges. Mike interviewed Antonio Carlos Jobim in a hotel on the Place des Vosges.

A piano teacher from Salt Lake City fooled Mike into thinking he was the friendly failed Mormon he pretended to be. He did not think learning music should be fun, and he was very cross when he discovered that Mike had been feeding Marcel unsavory morsels like "Blue Monk" and Mingus's "Nostalgia in Times Square." The Failed Mormon ordered Mike to cut it out—ordered, he wasn't kidding. Imagine interfering with his teaching method. Helping Marcel to learn those tunes had involved major intergenerational, bicultural bonding. Marcel was so quick to learn them, and they had laughed so much. Proud of themselves, they decided to fail the Failed Mormon. Later, they were to follow the score while listening to Stravinsky's "Le Sacré du Printemps" together, and to listen to *Abbey Road, Kind of Blue,* and *Gaucho* together. Major sacraments in the September of Mike's years.

Then, oddly enough, one October he went on the road with a rock band. It was kind of like running away with the circus. Going on the road is the answer to such metaphysical questions as what is the meaning of life, and does my wife love me? You are on hold: "Sorry, Mr. Rockefeller, I can't deal with my overdraft right now. I'm on the road." Politicians go on the campaign trail, dictators tour their provinces, young men ship out to sea, young women become airline stewardesses, working-class families take vacations in Winnebagos. Beatniks, of course, just went on the road. Alienation is no longer a problem on the road; you are alien everywhere.

Touring France, the French rock band Telephone had an English agent, English stage and tour managers, and English light and sound men using English hardware hauled in English lorries. French rock did not travel well, but Telephone sold millions of records at home. Their tour bus had a big "Starcruiser" painted on each side, and it was driven by an Englishman. "English road crews work twice as hard as the French and cost half as much," explained tour manager David Wernham. The band called him "Rostbif." There were bunks, a sound system, video, and a bar on the bus. It was the French rock tour of the year. They played arenas for eight thousand people in Montpélier, Nice, Lille, Grénoble, and Paris. Dressed in black and wearing a fedora, on top of a speaker pile, Mike played his trombone with a plunger on a song about a cat. Sixteen thousand hands clapping is nice to hear. You could smell the money flowing in. You could sniff it if you liked. On their way to Geneva, crossing a border for the first time, the singer, Jean-Louis Aubert, slipped Roastbif a small piece of paper folded like a drug package. "Do me a favor, David?" he said. "Hold this. You're so straight, they'll never search you." Flexing his road manager chops, Rostbif immediately threw it out the window. "Roxy Music pulled that on me years ago," he said.

Kids are considered good luck on the road. When Marcel, then about eight, came along for a hop, the members of Telephone, kids themselves, carried him on their shoulders and rolled around dressing room floors with him. They sat him onstage, just behind the drummer, Richard Kolinka. The music was so wondrously loud. Watching Kolinka toss and twirl his sticks, Marcel pointed to his own head and twisted his finger with admiration—he was really nuts, this guy. Kolinka painted his face like a pirate, and he painted Marcel too. Marcel tied a bandana like Richard's around his head and wherever Kolinka went, the kid he called "my shadow" was not far behind.

At the end of the tour, Mike asked Marcel to keep him company when he went to the office to get paid.

"You mean . . ." The kid hesitated: "You get *paid* to play music?"

It came as no surprise when he said he wanted to play the drums. A parent's nightmare. Unthinkable. Drums take up too much space, they are much too loud, and, as Chet Baker said, "It takes a pretty good drummer to be better than no drummer at all." As much as he disliked using Chet Baker as a lifestyle model, Mike cleverly talked Marcel out of the drums. It may have been sneaky, but he meant it. He said that the bass is a percussion instrument too, and "everybody needs a bass player." Which is true enough, although not quite so simple. Marcel bought it, he was a natural, and a year later, his electric bass slung low on his hip, he was singing "Hey Joe" with schoolmates in a cave near the Bastille. Parents and friends dropped francs into passed hats. Rehearsal studios and taxis were paid for. There was a growing investment in sound processing equipment — a drum machine, a mixing table, a sampler, a succession of basses.

When an offspring expresses interest in becoming a professional musician, throw a tantrum. Yell. All bets are off. Show no mercy. Take no prisoners. Disinherit. Tooling up can ruin your credit. The decibel level gets higher as the piano inevitably gives birth to that dreaded space invader called Keyboards, which will either be discarded in favor of a PlayStation or, worse, much worse, be loved and expanded. Digital technology permits infinite segues and textures and maximum volume with minimal effort. Your medieval music and dixieland archives will be drowned out by Jimi Hendrix and Bob Marley. If you're lucky, that is. If not, think Anthrax.

These days it can seem like all the lyrics have been written, and that the tunes have all been sung. Where are new licks going to come from? Western music as we know it seems just about played out. As he was nearing sixty, Beach Boy Brian Wilson said: "I think we've lost the ability to be blown away by music." Who will reinvent the Broadway song form? Choice mechanisms are drying up. Trends are by definition trendy. Where do Brazil, India, and Africa fit into the changing game? Are record companies still necessary? It's a tough time to be a young musician.

Planeland: Night. Terminal ennui. Mike and Marcel waiting for their late connecting flight to Paris from Minneapolis. This trip has been a tough haul—arriving on time for appointments with deans, teachers, and student advisers, asking pertinent questions, weighing alternatives. Figuring out the next step in the future of the child. Packing, unpacking, checking in and out of hotels, catching early morning flights, getting lost in rental cars in strip-malls in vaguely remembered cities. Planeland is plainly getting to Mike. He has just about abandoned all hope of leaving here. Stuck in a confluence of fear, frustration, anger, and boredom, he is overwhelmed by the cumulative dose of the banality, vulgarity, and all around ugliness of his native America. America makes his eyes hurt, his teeth ache, his ears whistle. American cities wither his soul. "New York is the most horrible place on God's earth," Henry Miller wrote in *The Air Conditioned Nightmare·* "No matter how many times I escape I am brought back, like a runaway slave, each time detesting it, loathing it, more and more." Miller's first visit to America after living in France and Greece "chilled me to the bone." This visit has chilled Mike to the bone. There is a lack of fresh air and sleep in Planeland. Drifting off into recollections of being on the road with Claude Thornhill's band, he is having doubts about the life he is steering his son into.

During a tour of Louisiana, Arkansas, Oklahoma, and states like that with Thornhill in the fifties, Mike's roomie, Squirms, invented a word game he called Roadopolis. Squirms was a road-rat with bleary eyes and a green complexion testifying to a dedicated pursuit of happiness. His definition of a square was someone who doesn't like to throw up. Squirms was laying low from the day. He said he had to jerk off to get his heart started in the morning. He consumed a succession of vials of vile liquids, and paper packages of illegal powders. When Squirms poured himself a taste from the flask he called his "band-aid"—a quadruple, four fingers, no fucking around—the smell of alcohol joined that of codeine cough syrup, and the dyspeptic cloud that surrounded him at all times. He looked like cat food. (Mike was allergic to cats.) Squirms hardly ever ate and yet he was overweight. If the gin people had added vitamins he would not have eaten at all.

Squirms inaugurated the game of Roadopolis on the outskirts of Odessa, Texas; the asshole of the world, he called it. It involved spotting wannabe corporate names like Bargaintown and Foam Rubber City. American entrepreneurs assume bloated identities they hope will put them on a larger map. Hamburgerburg, Kebab-bad (no shit), Toyville, Hush-Puppy Hollow, to say nothing of Disney World. Your average red-blooded American wants to be a Hummer—larger than life. The name of a store can cover square miles. Buy a soul in Shoe Village. It was the birth of the age of branding. Territorially ambitious names like Nike Town and Planet Hollywood have come to be called brand clusters. Marketing people call it "creating a destination." With Claude's four-hundred-mile hops between twofers in stale hick hotels, destinations were not lacking. Behind the wheel on a flat, two-lane road, Squirms stretched the envelope. "Dullsville," he said.

"Whacked Hollow," replied Mike.

Upon seeing a sexy woman in a rest stop: "Stacked Junction."

Seeing a pretty man: "Fagrad."

"Outasightistan" came to mind on the New Jersey Turnpike. The game was like a dumb pop song you can't get out of your head. Entering the Holland Tunnel, Squirms came up with the cosmically redundant "New York City *City*."

Back in Planeland: The connecting flight from Minneapolis has finally arrived. Boarding, Mike has become thoroughly spooked by the possible Squirmsization of Marcel. The dues he would pay for being a musician were on Mike's head.

Once he had taken the tyke—he must have been ten or eleven—along to an interview with Miles Davis. The Prince of Silence, or Darkness, take your pick, put a hand on Marcel's handsized head and croaked the question: "You going to be a musician like your old man?"

What was he supposed to say? "No"?

"Jazz thrived under Boss Pendergast's political machine in Kansas City when you played there in the 1930s," Mike said to Count Basie. *"How do you look back on that period?"*

"I'd like to tell you but I can't," Basie replied. *"I'm writing a book about my life and there are a lot of things I won't be able to tell you. We'll have to do a lot of curving."*

"OK. What's it like still having a successful big band now that big bands are supposed to be dead?"

"What do you mean 'What's it like'?"

"I mean, do you still enjoy it?"

"Of course. If I didn't have a band I'd be washing dishes. What else is there to do?"

"Other people have formed combos or moved to Vegas. There are alternatives."

"Maybe for some people. Not for me."

"What was Lester Young like when he joined you?"

"He was the same as always. Lester never changed."

"You know you shouldn't be afraid to tell me things that will be in your book. This will help promote it."

"I'm not afraid to tell you. I'm just not going to tell you."

Mike's face got red.

"Now don't go getting red in the face . . ."

Losing his temper, Mike got up to leave, and said: "Let's forget the whole thing."

"Well, don't lose your temper." The Kid from Red Bank hung his mouth

open in surprise: "You're the first journalist that ever acted that way with me."

"It's just not worth it."

"Come on. Sit down. I just said that I can't tell you and you took offense."

"Yes I did," said Mike, sitting down.

"That's where you were wrong. You should have asked me another question and then come back to it. I would have answered you. You mustn't always be looking for something bad like that to happen. If you do, any little thing is likely to get to you and bad things will happen. Don't look for reasons to be unhappy. I don't. Ever. All down through my life, no matter what went wrong, I always felt all right. That way nobody nowhere on earth can ever offend me. I try to get along with everybody and everything."

"So what was Kansas City like under the Pendergast machine in the 1930s?" Mike asked again.

Basie laughed and said: "I can see that you are going to fool around and try and trick me into telling you anyway. I can see that."

4

THE SLUSH PUMP AND THE SILENT LETTER

WHAT DO YOU CALL A TROMBONE PLAYER WITHOUT A
GIRLFRIEND?
   HOMELESS.

—MUSICIAN'S JOKE

J. J. Johnson told Mike that he wondered what could have been going through his mind when, in an Indianapolis high school, he volunteered to play the trombone.

"What attracted me to it?" he asked rhetorically. "The trombone is the most ungainly, awkward, beastly hard instrument you can imagine."

Any musical instrument nicknamed "slush pump" cannot be considered sexy. Mike passed the entrance examination to the High School of Music and Art, on top of a hill in Harlem, on the accordion. Players of non-orchestral instruments had to learn one. He had long arms and fleshy lips, and so they gave him a trombone, and he began to pump in front rather than sideways.

The tone of the trombone, which is produced by blowing into a tube unimpeded by mechanical or electronic devices, has been described as the closest sound to the human voice. Practicing such an ungainly, awkward, beastly instrument takes extreme dedication and a well-developed sense of irony. This can be an attractive combination in a man. Plus the long arms and fleshy lips. Educated, willowy, ironic women often go for trombone players. "I used to be married to a trombone player" are encouraging words. Brahms called it "the voice of God."

The trombone's ancestor the sackbut was a part of ceremonial bands as far back as the fourteenth century. In 1495, Henry VII engaged four *shakbusshes* for his castle band. Olivier de la Marche's memoirs refer to a *trompette-saicqueboute* used in a motet played at the wedding of the Duke of Burgundy and Margaret of York at Bruges in 1468. Sackbut chorales were played from sixteenth-century German church towers. Monteverdi wrote for five trombones in his opera *Orfeo*. Handel scored for the instrument. There is a prominent trombone solo during the supper scene in Mozart's *Don Giovanni*. Mike played the trombone solo in Mozart's Requiem Mass with the High School of Music and Art symphony orchestra. Beethoven, Wagner, and Berlioz added more trombones, and gave them more exposure. Berlioz said that the instrument could portray everything from "religious accent, calm and imposing, to wild clamors of the orgy." "With its formidable reserve of power," Anthony C. Baines wrote in the *New Grove Dictionary*, "it is not surprising that the trombone was sometimes used as if loudness were its main attribute." Felix Mendelssohn said it was "too sacred for frequent use."

It does not look sacred. Tubes stick out in front and back. Spit accumulates in them, and the emptying of spit is a prime skill on the instrument. Trombonists blow spitballs at orchestra mates through their unimpeded tubes. They bump into things. Trombone slides have been known to kill instrumentalists standing too close in front of them. In turn-of-the-twentieth-century New Orleans parades, the only place it was safe to play the trombone was on the end of the wagon—the style became known as "tailgate." Jack Teagarden, Dickie Wells, and Trummie Young made the trombone respectable in the front line. J. J. gave it speed and elegance.

"J. J. Johnson is to his horn what Charlie Parker and Dizzy Gillespie were to theirs," Stanley Crouch wrote in the *Village Voice*. "His work had the dreamy smoothness heard in Lester Young, the crackle of Roy Eldridge's fourth-gear lyricism, the rhythmically intricate contempt espoused by Parker for the limitations of articulation and the gnarled wit of Gillespie." Crouch could be full of shit. He could also be violent. Quoting Crouch makes Mike uncomfortable.

Jimmy Knepper, whose trombone was one of Charles Mingus's emblems, can be said to have added a fifth gear. Knepper was as essential to Mingus—and, to a lesser degree, to Gil Evans—as Johnny Hodges was to Duke Ellington, Freddie Green to Count Basie, Tex Beneke to Glenn Miller. Knepper said it was too bad that Glenn Miller's music didn't die instead of Glenn Miller. Along with Kai Winding, he developed his own distinct bebop voice. Combining the clarity, daring, and precision of J. J. with the lyricism of Teagarden and Wells, his virtuoso articulation involved creative false positioning, finding notes on the horn where they had no business being, and a sound close to the God of your choice.

Mike played second trombone to Knepper's lead during a tour of Switzerland and Germany by the George Gruntz Concert Jazz Band. Elvin Jones played drums. Elvin's style was based on multidirectional drumming and surging over bar lines, which is fine when you're playing with John Coltrane, but a drummer in a big band is something like an orchestra conductor. One part of the job is to make sure everybody knows where "one" is. After leaving Coltrane in 1966, Elvin was hired by Duke Ellington. For reasons never explained to him, but having to do with either rhythmic (multidirectional drumming) or political (new guy on the block) ambiguity, Ellington also kept his previous drummer on the payroll. Elvin called it "one of my least pleasant musical experiences."

With Gruntz, when Elvin once chose to come off a roll on two instead of one, the ensemble got screwed up, and Knepper rose out of his seat and looked under and behind chairs and risers, asking: "Where's one? I can't find one. Anybody know where one is?" This was onstage, in front of a live audience.

Elvin said he "could never understand how people could have trouble comprehending my time. I never thought I was being all that complex. It's all about paying attention to other people, and supporting what they are doing. I'm still wrestling to control my own impulses—you know, trying to avoid hitting everything at once." He called it "de-emphasizing" the strong beat. The critic Leonard Feather described Elvin's time as "a continuum in which no beat of the bar was necessarily indicated by any specific accent."

Asked where the fifteen hundred students who enrolled in one of his percussion clinics in Japan were going to find work, Elvin smiled, and his strong black face, along with the room itself, lit up, and he said: "You don't have to win the Tour de France to enjoy riding a bicycle." As a young man, Elvin worked in a steel mill in Pontiac, Michigan, "pouring molten iron out of a Bessemer converter. It could be dangerous work, partly because it is so repetitive. The biggest risk is losing your concentration. Kind of like drumming. A guy named Horse worked at the mill. Horse would drink a pint of Old Grand-Dad with the sandwich in his lunch pail. He said it kept the dust off his lungs. He could handle it. Whether it's a steel mill or a jazz band, relating to human beings involves basic truths, positive and negative. They have never changed and never will change. That's why I read poetry. It's universal. That's why I play music."

At dawn one morning with Gruntz, the English saxophonist Alan Skidmore walked into the breakfast room of a hotel in Zurich where Elvin, Howard Johnson, John Scofield, Woody Shaw, Knepper, Mike, and some others were only half awake. Skid bopped right over, put his coke-bottle eyeglasses into Elvin's face, and said: "Elvin, it sure is a pleasure to wake up in the morning and see *you*."

Knepper's, on the other hand, was a face you generally did not want to see. He was the sort of person who could say, on being invited to dinner: "No thanks. I think I'll go up to my room and mope." He was a moper. Gruntz's compositions had a tendency to keep changing time signatures as in classical music, instead of specifying the accents in 4/4 like a jazz arranger would do. Knepper kept complaining about them. He considered the string of time signature changes to be an unnecessary, flagrant example of European pseudo-gravitas. Gruntz was Swiss. His arrangements drove Knepper around the bend. After playing a composition in which the time kept going back and forth in differing permutations between three, four, five, six, and seven, Knepper spent the intermission with his nose to the music, counting furiously, his finger tracing the staffs. Finally, triumphantly, he exclaimed: "Just as I thought. There are exactly sixty-four bars of 4/4 between B and C." Knepper had the sort of eccentric creativity you might expect from someone who played a clumsy device called the slush pump, and whose name began with a silent letter.

When the young Glenn Ferris, later to become one of Knepper's most accomplished successors, introduced himself to Freddie Hubbard, he said: "I'm a trombone player." The trumpet star instinctively replied: "That's tough."

There will never be a statue of Glenn Ferris erected in France. Not that he necessarily deserves it. It's just a way to say that the French will never erect a statue to honor a white jazz musician. (Except, of course, a *French* white jazz musician.) There was a larger-than-life statue of Wynton Marsalis in Marciac in the Gers in southwestern France. Wynton performed every summer at the

Jazz in Marciac festival. Thanks in large part to him, jazz had become essential to this disadvantaged farming town's economic health. Wynton loved the area's good food and wine. He liked the producer and approved of his programming, and the locals appreciated Wynton's charm and cache of fame. He was a hero to the kids he taught at the local jazz school the festival had spawned. Wynton was very good at teaching children. However, the fact remains that he would not have enjoyed a larger-than-life-statue level of respect if he were not African-American. (There was also a statue of Sidney Bechet on the Côte d'Azur.) Being handsome, energetic, creative, and charming would not have been enough.

Not that it was Wynton's fault, but in France, white American jazz musicians were seen as not being quite authentic. Ferris—among the best, let's say, five trombonists in the world—was in two worst-possible worlds. Although he had lived in France for decades, spoke French, and was married to a French woman, he would always be a foreigner. In Amsterdam, once a musician of any race had invested in settling there, and learned the laws and the language, he was considered Dutch. In the U.S., a Russian could come to New York and, if he could play, he became just a cat with a funny accent. Meanwhile, having left, Ferris had become a foreigner in the U.S. also. He never entered even the bottom rungs of the *Down Beat* jazz poll. "I find the degree to which I am unspoken of in America rather extreme," Ferris said.

Having worked with, among others, Stevie Wonder, the Beach Boys, the Brecker Brothers, Tim Buckley, Harry James, Art Pepper, the Average White Band, James Taylor, Billy Cobham, George Duke, Buddy Miles, Don Ellis, and Frank Zappa's Mothers of Invention, Ferris had pretty much exhausted work possibilities in Los Angeles. It was time to move on. A short stay in New York turned out to be only a pit stop on the way to Paris.

Not coincidentally, a few years after Ferris arrived, Mike

switched from the trombone to its cousin the bass trumpet. It had the same mouthpiece, and you can be surer of at least getting close to the notes by pressing valves rather than positioning a slide. Little by little, he played less trombone and became a would-be full-time bass trumpeter. A bass trumpet is not merely a marching band instrument like a valve trombone, which also has the same mouthpiece as a slush pump. Except when played by Bob Brookmeyer, valve trombones tend to sound stuffed up, out of tune, and vulgar. Mike's expensive, hand-built bass trumpet had a sound with a lot of core to it. In the upper register, it was not unlike a flugelhorn. His bass trumpet was built to play Berlioz and Respighi, both of whom wrote for the instrument. Being a full-time journalist, Mike had become a part-time trombonist, and the instrument is too difficult to play part-time. Even a bass trumpet is too difficult to play part-time. Paris was not big enough for two white American trombone players when one of them was as good as Glenn Ferris.

The golden age of Americans in Paris may have been over, but back home, deep down, a lot of Americans in creative lines of work remained jealous of the dirty rats who had deserted a sinking ship, and, instead of drowning as expected, were sailing along quite nicely thank you very much on a cleaner and less mean steamer. A Parisian critic called Ferris the "Stan Getz of the trombone."

Arriving in Paris, Ferris played Haitian music in dancehalls where the music went pretty much nonstop from eleven to five. It was a good workout, and good exposure. The leader of Galaxy, a successful Paris-based group from Guadeloupe, offered him an apartment and a guaranteed salary to come back and play and arrange for them. He could not refuse. At first, he went to the movies alone, walked a lot, visited museums. It was lonely, but he was seduced. He began to make a living in Germany, Switzerland, Holland, Italy, Spain, and Japan as a sideman, sub, and eventually guest star. He became a leader with five different formations playing his own music. There were no top-forty hits, and he could not afford roadies, but he earned enough to buy property in the up-scale exurb of Chantilly. The odds against such success in such a business in such a place on such an instrument are long.

"People don't want to see and hear trombone players fighting their slides," Ferris said. "Saxophones and trumpets don't have that problem. The audience becomes too conscious that you are play-ing a 'difficult' instrument. They just want to be carried away by music."

Ferris could carry you away. Still, the image problem remained. The trombone will always be something of a joke.

What is the height of optimism?

A trombone player with a beeper.

What do you call a woman who is on the arm of a trombone player?

A tattoo.

What's the difference between a frog and a trombone player crossing the road?

The frog is going to a gig.

A trombone player's car is stolen, and the police call to say they found it. Praying that his expensive German horn is still inside, the trombonist rushes down to claim the car. He opens the trunk with trepidation. To find—two trombones.

Barbershops & Whorehouses IV

Music should be judged on its own terms.
—*Elvin Jones*

5

TIMOTHY LEARY
VOLTAGE SMART

YOUNG PEOPLE SHOULD BE SEEN AND NOT HEARD,
BECAUSE THEY'RE GOOD-LOOKING BUT NOT TOO BRIGHT.
WE'RE PRETTY BRIGHT BY NOW, BUT WE'RE UGLY.
—GRACE SLICK, 2003

Mike was stuck in Paris. Which was better than being stuck in, say, Algiers.

It's hard not to be stuck somewhere—stuck in real life, dealing with social benefits, utility bills, taxes, plumbers. Marie-France hooked Mike up with her plumber when he had a leak. Taking out his wrenches, the plumber asked him how come they were married and lived in two different places.

"She's my almost sort-of ex-wife," Mike said. "We're buddies. It's complicated."

The plumber wrenched and looked knowingly at Mike, and said, man-to-man, that he had two ex-wives in different apartments around Paris, and he was friendly with both of them. Not to say anything nice about the French, but Mike had good luck with French plumbers.

Being stuck in a place you like, doing something you want to do, was a sort of libertarian house arrest—not all that bad, but stuck is stuck. Mike absolutely had to hang on to his French health insurance and, like most journalists, he was totally hooked on his byline. Everybody likes to see his name in the paper. And then there's the place itself. If New York is technology's victory over man, then Paris is man's victory over technology. At a cocktail party one Saturday night on Île St. Louis, a teenage girl came up to him and said that her mother—she pointed to a woman in a corner—had told her that Mike had played with Miles Davis. Was it true?

He said that it was.

"When was that?" she asked.

"Nineteen forty-eight," he replied. He'd seen that look before. "I know, I know," he said. "You weren't born yet."

She looked over at her mother again, and then it hit him, and Mike said: "You mean your *mother* wasn't born yet?"

He'd better get used to it. It was not going to get any better.

Young people think that old people wear old people masks—that they had worn their *real* faces when they were young. Young people look in the mirror and wonder how they will look wearing their old person's mask. But when you actually get to be old, it turns out that the young face was the mask. Some young people already wear old faces. Was it Camus who said that everybody over forty is responsible for his own face?

The French media have a kind of gentlemen's agreement to dumb down Saturday night television. There are only game shows and reality programs on the national stations. The cable runs bad B-movies dubbed into French, or, more irritatingly, good movies by people like Bergman and Fellini dubbed into French, just in case you were tempted to stay in and watch the tube. It is a conspiracy to get people to go out and spend money at least one night a week. Social democracy at work. Saturday night is amateur night.

Musicians rarely go out on Saturday night, unless they have a gig. In his winter years, Mike took to going to bed with a good book on Saturday night. The problem was that a good book would no longer keep him awake for long. There was no point resisting. Even his naps had naps. "How good it is to slip into the brief oblivion of sleep," Alexander Solzhenitsyn wrote about the ease of taking naps in old age: "And what a gift to wake once more in the clarity of your second or third morning of the day."

Slipping into oblivion watching default cable one Saturday night, Mike chanced upon a documentary film on Canal Jimmy — a nice name for a French TV channel—about the death of Timothy Leary. It was like a slow-motion replay of a two-minute warning period in a lopsided football game, from the point of view of the loser. Leary was terminally ill from the opening credits. Time was cosmically out. Sudden-death. Leary was all pumped up. Nothing was going to save his ass but a Hail Mary.

Speaking on-camera to bedside friends and chroniclers about having terminal cancer, Leary updated his patented metaphysical raps with a new one about death. Death, he said, was the ultimate out of body experience. Good old Tim, a drug fan until the end.

He had lost his hair, and his eyes were deep-set and just about out of sight in his hollow face. His body was paper-thin. At the end of the documentary he died, and the doctors sawed off his head and put it in a jar so his brain could be frozen for posterity. No shit. That may sound spooky, but Leary had a healthy ego and a really first-class smile, and he was sure that it was all well worth preserving. Anyway, it was also a good hustle. The filmmakers paid his medical costs in return for the film rights. It took place in Los Angeles.

Mike had left New York to become the European editor of the *Village Voice* on January 20th, 1969, Richard Nixon's first inauguration day. It was not entirely coincidental. Obviously, the American government could not get any worse. (He was wrong.) He had no contract; it was understood to be for two or three years. It didn't matter, he was just glad—he was surprised how glad—to leave America. Strange that he should feel this way about his native country. He began to travel so often to so many places in Europe, Asia, and Africa, with so many languages, currencies, male and female plugs, and electrical currents, that he began to think of himself as Voltage Smart (a good name for a rock band), like his laptop.

In Swinging London, his Bulgarian girlfriend gave him a threesome for his fortieth birthday. He was fucking Irish twins who lived in Belgravia; they liked to play with his head and he could never be sure which was which. He made it with his landlady, his literary agent, an airline stewardess, and a Hollywood producer's wife. Although there were also good music and good drugs, as has been said about Hollywood, Swinging London was mostly about pussy. It was not about contemplation.

Mike moved to Paris one right-hand-drive Beetle-load at a time. Driving a right-handed Volkswagen Beetle convertible with English plates in France was very voltage smart. Talk about the margin. He met Marie-France when she was the token woman in the office of the underground magazine *Actuel.* Her boss Jean-François was the Jerry Rubin of France. Or was it the Abbie Hoffman? No, that was Jean-Jacques. Keeping all those French hyphenated given names—Jean-Pierre, Jean-Marie, Pierre-Henri, Michel-Antoine— straight was like adding up the number ninety-nine. Four times twenty plus ten plus nine. French is not a language that prides itself on its simplicity. You have to figure four numbers to get one, remember two names for one.

It was either Jean-François or Jean-Jacques who gave Mike Timothy Leary's number in Algeria, where Leary was good and stuck at the moment. Mike had been introduced to him by Maynard Ferguson, with whom he'd played the trombone for a minute. Maynard had been in on some early acid tests. Now Leary was on the run.

The *Voice* had been nagging their European editor to go and report on Northern Ireland, which was literally exploding. But there were already enough journalists sniffing around up there. Mike was not going to fight for a place on that long line. He was looking for the holes in the Swiss cheese. "The holes in your Swiss cheese are somebody else's Swiss cheese," his friend Hamburger had said. If Northern Ireland was then the big cheese in the news, Timothy Leary in Algeria was a significant hole in it. One wire-service reporter told Mike that his article *A Revolutionary Bust,* date-lined Algiers, was "the biggest story since Jerry Garcia first dropped acid."

Leary had escaped from a Californian prison, where he was serving time for something like corrupting American youth. He and his partner Rosemary Woodruff—both fugitives; she'd helped him escape—surfaced in Algiers. Not having an alternative, they'd put themselves "under the protection of" (Leary's words) Eldridge Cleaver and the Black Panther "embassy." Other liberation fronts, the Ethiopian for example, had embassies in Algiers in the early nineteen-seventies. Algeria was the only country that did not consider them terrorists. They were all good and stuck there.

Cleaver and Leary both considered themselves to be leaders of major international cultural revolutions. While it lasted, their confrontation was, if not quite hard news, at least solid news. Both were wanted men in America. Oversimplifying the matter, but not by much, Mike figured that the city of Algiers was just not big enough to hold the two of them. It was a micro civil war. Cleaver was in the process of coinventing what came to be known as radical chic. Leary, always good copy, continually stretching the envelope, with an outlandish tongue and a planet-sized ego, was handsome, lucid, funny, fearless, and usually stoned. Mike was fond of him.

When he called Algiers from Paris, Leary answered the phone and said sure, come down: "We'll pick you up at the airport." In fact, Mike was met by a surly African American who did not introduce himself and asked a lot of personal questions. He said that the Learys had had a prior engagement and please get in the car. Under a bright blue sky, they drove through the white Mediterranean city and into suburban hills, arriving at a high-rent, high-rise seaside apartment building. Leary was at the front door of his large and airy flat. Mike asked him what was going on. Hugging him, wearing that well-worn shit-eating grin of his, Leary replied: "It seems that we are under arrest. And now, presumably, so are you."

It was a benevolent detention. Timothy and Rosemary were bright-eyed, suntanned, well fed, and the Panther guards seemed more bored than unfriendly. Cleaver was accusing Leary of "compromising security" by entertaining visitors carrying drugs to get their guru high. He was right—Leary was being extremely uncool. Cleaver called it a "revolutionary bust." After being restricted to the apartment for two days, they were permitted an unchaperoned drive to a nearby beach. Cleaver was not taking much of a risk. Leary had literally no place to run. Two Greek hippies introduced themselves on the beach, and everybody had a smoke. Leary said he wished he could get Cleaver stoned because "Eldridge is way too uptight."

They both agreed to tape a debate for the *Village Voice*. Full of aggression, without self-doubt, the dialogue centered on the need for, and the nature of, revolution. Words kept coming back—"pig," "man," "righteous," "downer," "right-on." Was it more important to free our minds or our bodies? Who were more oppressed, hippies or blacks? They both took themselves quite seriously. Talking like entrepreneurs, each defending his own interests, they were energetic, sincere, dedicated, unquestioning. Who could have guessed how out-to-lunch that dialogue would come to sound? It was some sort of hippie *Spinal Tap*.

Mike went to the central post office in downtown Algiers to call his editors at the *Voice*, and tell them about his scoop. He was feeling good about himself. Having no local money, he called collect. There was a two-hour wait for an overseas line. It was hot, and very damp, and it smelled like an unwashed armpit in the central post office. His collect call was refused. It turned out that the editor had been waging a campaign against unnecessary phone expenses. A collect call from Algeria? Certainly not. The editor apologized later. Still, "A Revolutionary Bust" was buried on page twenty-seven.

After Mike left, Leary and Rosemary broke out, after which they broke up. Leary had further adventures in Switzerland involving a younger and richer lover, a Porsche convertible, and a screen test for a starring role in the movie of *Steppenwolf*. On the post-Panther lam, Leary was being handed from one Swiss canton to another on a series of three-month subleases. He drove his sports car around the Alps, the long blond hair of his new woman blowing in the wind. Not a care in the world. He was a star. Swiss hippies provided him with acid. When he met Dr. Hoffman, the Swiss inventor of LSD, there were articles about it in the local papers. Leary flunked his screen test for *Steppenwolf*, then in preproduction in Basel. Fishman, the producer, was a fan of his, and Leary's test was not bad, but he was not thought to be directable; and, star or not, he was not bankable. This was an uninsurable renegade dope fiend wanted by the FBI and Interpol. Max von Sydow got the part. More about that later. Leary was arrested by Interpol trying to go through Pakistani customs.

Watching his death documentary by default on Canal Jimmy,

Mike heard Leary's version of the end of the Algerian episode for the first time. Alerted by the press, Leary said, the government told the Black Panthers that they had no right to arrest anybody in Algeria. This was not their country, and they had better all start thinking seriously about getting their sorry, stuck asses out of there.

Barbershops & Whorehouses   V

I am not a socialist, I am not a capitalist. I am a saxophonist.
—Janos, a Polish jazz musician

6

JAZZ IN SIBERIA

LEFT-HANDED TIMES

PRISONERS WERE BROUGHT IN, AND ONE, COMPLETELY
FIT, WAS THEN SHOT AND WOUNDED TWICE BY A RED
ARMY MAN FOR NO REASON AT ALL. THE POLE WRITHED
AND GROANED, AND THEY PUT A PILLOW UNDER HIS
HEAD.
—ISAAC BABEL, *1920 DIARY*

One nice thing about being stuck in Paris was how easy it was to
get out of. Where Paris was was a big part of what it was. Which
may sound like a left-handed compliment, but it was not meant
that way, and, anyhow, Mike was living in left-handed times.

During the early days of perestroika, a letter arrived from a Mad
Russian of Mike's acquaintance informing him that his plans for a
Tashkent Jazz Festival were now "misty."

"The date moves maybe to next year, or even another city," the
letter went on: "Like in that known joke—everything is accurately
right except not he but she, not wins but loses, not money but husband. I will send you a detailed message to persuade Herald and his
Trombone to criticize the swinging camels who are jazzin' up our
perestroika."

That seemed to be that. Then an invitation arrived by cable and it turned out to be not Tashkent but Novosibirsk, not a festival but a "Symposium of New Music."

Gold Valley 88 was held from May 11 to 15, 1988, in a think tank called Akademgorodok (Academy Town), a self-contained complex of sad but not poor medium-rise buildings in a birch forest in the exurbs of Novosibirsk. The population of a hundred thousand consisted of the academic community and those who serviced it. It had been founded thirty years earlier by scientists with pioneering spirits who first saw this dip in the steppe in the autumn when the trees are a riot of color, and named it Gold Valley. Professor Abel Aganbegyan, founder of the Siberian Institute of Economics, had been advocating economic reform from his post in Akademgorodok since the 1960s. He had been a leading opponent of the plan to reverse the flow of Siberian rivers. Gorbachev brought Aganbegyan to Moscow as a high-level adviser. Tatiana Zaslavskaya, Aganbegyan's student and successor as the institute's director, wrote a paper in 1983 calling for more market forces and less planning in the Soviet economy. She, too, became a senior Gorbachev aide. Residents called Akademgorodok the Russian Cambridge. Which one was not specified.

Perestroika notwithstanding, it was not totally clear if the Second Symposium of New Music was strictly kosher. Producer Sergei Belichenko covered his dubious tracks with a clean letterhead, calling his organizing committee "The Center of Studies on Folklore Activity and Cultural Public Education." He made it clear that this was a symposium that had nothing to do with the threatening Americano-bourgeois music that both Hitler and Stalin banned. Have a nice day, *Monsieur le Ministre.* Interviewed in the book *Russian Jazz, New Identity,* Belichenko said: "I think that avant-garde jazz is one of the most significant artistic phenomena of the century. I do not accept that it should be called 'black music'—the music is above all such ethnic criteria." Wynton Marsalis would not approve.

After Pat Metheny toured the Soviet Union in 1987, he said: "I went where I liked and saw and talked to whomever I wanted. I was almost disappointed with the absence of the 'intrigue factor.'" Arriving in Moscow's Sheremetyevo International Airport with a journalist's visa and carrying a double trombone case the size of a small coffin, Mike felt like a walking intrigue factor. It turned out that he was only one more traveler arriving in a foreign airport with nobody to meet him. The absence of intrigue was almost insulting. He could have used a good intriguer to deal with the horde of taxi drivers trying to hustle the drive to Vnukovo Airport, where he had what might be loosely defined as a connecting flight to Novosibirsk.

Midnight. The small Vnukovo canteen was empty except for Mel, Mike, alluring Alicia, and two tired stewardesses. Mike knew his name was Mel because he had a T-shirt with "MEL" on it. A member of a church choir traveling around singing for peace, Mel was on his way from Seattle to catch up with his chorale in Omsk. His church had a long name Mike did not recognize. Mel said his church did not believe in hell because their doctrine holds that hell is here and now.

Alluring Alicia was gliding around the transit area wearing earphones and a Walkman and an alluring look on her face. She looked like Julie Christie, but not quite. When Mike asked her what she was listening to, she said "Gabor Szabo"—a Hungarian guitar player. If you think that's strange, you should know that she lived in Brasilia and was on her way to Lvov to visit her parents; that her Brazilian husband was in Beirut at the moment; and that Alluring Alicia spoke Arabic but not Portuguese.

Flying over four time zones, Mike landed in Novosibirsk at eight o'clock in the morning. He was met by gynecologist, drummer, festival promoter, and genial host Belichenko, also known as the "Siberian Norman Granz." Belichenko had recently told a Polish magazine: "I dream someday of forming a Siberian Jazz Association. And then maybe an Asian Association." He opened up his attaché case, took out a bottle—the only thing in it—and offered Mike a taste of "Moldavian Moonshine." Gorbachev was encouraging Russians to buy less vodka and people were busy making it in their bathtubs. Belichenko was responsible for bringing two hundred musicians, jazz critics, and miscellaneous experts from many time zones to Akademgorodok. A Lithuanian reedman said, in English, that the very idea of a Siberian jazz festival was "mind-blowing."

Daytime seminars dealt with such topics as "The Aesthetics of New Jazz." The blues and bebop were rare during the evening concerts. This jazz was *new*. Except for Mike and Conrad Bauer, an East German trombonist, the participants were all from the disintegrating Soviet Union, maybe half from Siberia.

Gold Valley 88 was staged in Science House, a modern, well-maintained office building and cultural center with a thousand-seat auditorium and a lush atrium overflowing with a variety of trees and flowers. You might wonder just what these scientists were growing there. And why. Arkhangelsk, a band from the Arctic city of the same name, unfurled a banner with the word "glasnost" in Russian but without vowels in it while they were improvising abstractly. In Russian, "glasnost" means "vowel" as well as "openness"; the absence of vowels implied openness without freedom. "Theoretically we have always had freedom of speech, even under Stalin," said keyboardist Vladimir Turov. "We wanted to remind people that you have to work for freedom. We had doubts about the banner, and there were long discussions before the concert, but jazz is a cry for freedom and we wanted to express something of our history through our performance."

Mikhail Alperin, a Jewish pianist from Moldova—then still called Moldavia—played a solo set mixing his ethnic roots with elements of ragtime, Bartók, and snatches of *Caravan* and Bud Powell's *Parisian Thoroughfare*. Bands from Tomsk, Kemerovo, Talin, Moscow, and Leningrad had better intentions than execution, but quality was not the point. Jazz was a common metaphor for freedom. These people did not gather together very often, certainly not in Siberia.

Slavic, pale, short, short-haired, the fast-talking hipster Belichenko arranged a late party for a few of the male visitors in a sauna on an army base a half-hour drive from Science House. They were sitting around naked, wiping their sweat with white bath towels. There was black bread, sausage, cheese, and spit-roasted chickens to accompany the jug of rose-colored Moldavian Moonshine labeled "Benzina" that was passed around. When it was empty, somebody asked if there was any more. "Oceans," was the reply.

You did not buy Moldavian Moonshine, you scored it. As oceans continued to flow, the conversation in the sauna grew more animated, the laughter more hysterical. Jokes were exchanged. A journalist from Kiev asked what was the difference between the Soviet Union before and after Gorbachev. The answer was: "Before, if you were standing on the street with a bottle of vodka and a foreign newspaper and a policeman appeared, you would hide the newspaper and drink. Now you hide the bottle and read."

Within the context of the sweating, drunken, towel-wrapped conviviality, Mike assumed the irony would be obvious when his turn came to propose a toast, and he said: "To the Evil Empire." A pall descended, and a critic from Leningrad said: "I hope this won't shock you, but I think your President Reagan was right. It was an evil empire. Rarely has a government been so far from its own people as we were under Brezhnev."

"Was? Were?" Belichenko objected.

Whatever new openings there may or may not have been socially or intellectually, the physical was even grungier than when Mike had toured the Soviet Union with the Earl "Fatha" Hines band twenty years earlier. Akademgorodok was a privileged place for a scientific elite, and a Westerner accustomed to cold climes would have felt only marginally uncomfortable. But the Soviet reality hit hard one evening when a group of festival guests drove the thirty-five kilometers to Novosibirsk, which then had a population of close to two million. All of a sudden, the movie went black and white. Pointing to the lines of people outside the stores, Belichenko said: "You do not go shopping in Novosibirsk, you go hunting." The air reeked of cheap diesel oil. There were plenty of smokestacks, and no trees. A restaurant they chose to go to—in fact, the only one open—was a realization of your worst Socialist nightmare. It reeked of boredom, filth, lack of proportion, and terminal hopelessness. Platters of cold meat awaiting them on a crumby and unwashed tablecloth looked as though they had been there for days. The lack of style and anything approaching civility, the unrelenting ugliness of Soviet life, embarrassed the Russians in the party. A trombonist from Perm said that Soviet trombones made good fishing poles, and, over stale herring, a photographer from Krasnodar said that Soviet cameras were great for hammering nails.

Hustling his symposium, working within the parameters of perestroika, Belichenko picked up a newly semiprivatized sponsor —Vega, a manufacturer of sound reproduction equipment. Vega's wares were displayed in the lobby of the steel and concrete concert hall. One of their models featured twin cassette decks. Having been told that you have to get a key from a party official to make a photocopy, Mike asked a dumb question: "How come you can copy spoken words but not printed words?"

"I never thought of that," Belichenko replied.

A colorful painting of a friendly oversized bear on a banner hung over the stage, along with the slogan (in English) "Peace, Love and Jazz Supreme." Orchestrion, a trio from Volgagrad (formerly Stalingrad) played in front of a larger-than-life slide projection of a man proudly displaying a portrait of Stalin tattooed on his chest. Orchestrion played with something close to desperation. Mike was told that Volgagrad is a "militaristic" and "patriotic" city, still clinging to the glory of victory in World War II. Orchestrion were not exactly hometown heroes.

What was called "new jazz" in the Soviet Union was explosive music with a minimum of rules in which emotion and symbolism took precedence over technique and tradition. Like free jazz with black power, Russian new jazz could not be separated from politics. Its audience was small, intellectual, linked to the plastic arts, and critical of the system. Vladimir Tarasov compared the situation to free jazz in New York in the sixties. One of the best percussionists in the USSR, he was also a painter and was known for his collection of contemporary Soviet art. He was both an art and a jazz critic. The following week he would perform a solo percussion piece at the Kunstmuseum in Bern, Switzerland, as part of an exhibition called "Moscow Artists of the '80s." Living in a large wooden house on two hectares of forest land seventy kilometers from Vilnius, he owned two boats and a car. Tarasov worked more in New York than in Siberia. In Akademgorodok, he began a solo concert with a tape playing militant Socialist songs from the 1930s. Then he switched on a rhythm box programmed to parody military marches. Joining in on his drum kit, he moved from melodic to rhythmic accents and back again, weaving in and out of the revolutionary songs with provocative intensity. It was an aural equivalent of the Stalin tattoo.

Vladimir Chekasin had just been voted the most popular jazz musician in the Soviet Union. He and Tarasov had both been members of the Vyacheslav Ganelin Trio. Ganelin described their successful style as "closer to contemporary chamber music than free jazz." The German critic Joachim-Ernst Berendt called it the "wildest yet best organized" free jazz he'd ever heard. Saxophonist Checkasin, who has been called the "Jacques Tati of jazz," closed the festival with a ballet he had conceived. A compact, volatile, enigmatic figure with brooding eyes, he moved his face and body like a mime, jerked like a robot on wires, posed as a dixieland clarinetist, raced through chords like Cannonball Adderley, imitated a breathy Coleman Hawkins, and played two saxophones at the same time like Rahsaan Roland Kirk. The Russian critic Efim Barban had written of Chekasin: "Reality sometimes appears in his music as a distorted caricature reflection of the fictitious, as a sham, so that what it excludes as fictitious becomes the true, authentic reality."

For four days most of the music had been without key signatures, swing, bar lines, or recognizable melodies. Mike tried to play Charlie Parker's "Buzzy" with a Siberian rhythm section, but the blues were not alive and well in Siberia.

All of that is, of course, historical toast. But if books can be written and films can be made about, for example, the Beatles, and the birth of the blues, Soviet jazz deserves at least a chapter. And if you think that's a stretch, how about Soviet beauty care?

"Siberia" (in English) was the name of a cooperative that Gold Valley's associate producer Alyosha Krestianov had incorporated a few months earlier. Its slogan was "Beauty and Health for Women." Private cooperatives were a central element in the Gorbachev economic restructuring program. A hairdresser by trade, Krestianov threw a lunch and cocktail party in his apartment in Akademgorodok (he was the town coiffeur) after the festival. His partners included professional beauty care experts and their idea was to offer "any service a woman needs to ease her nonprofessional life—diagnoses, massage, acupuncture, and beauty care and products."

The English name was chosen with an eye toward eventual exports of perfumes, creams, and balms to the West. How anybody could think that the name "Siberia" represented an attractive image of clean air, wooded mountains, and ecological correctness is a good question. This was not Quebec. The marketing plan included providing shopping services along with beauty treatments. During a toast, Krestianov announced that deals were being negotiated with stores so that the cooperative's workers would go out and buy groceries in supermarkets for their clients while they were being treated in Siberia's beauty shops.

"Nyet, nyet," shouted Belichenko: "There are no supermarkets." He was suffering from a combination of postfestival depression and massive doses of Moldavian Moonshine. "There are no beauty shops. So far this cooperative does nothing but spend money."

"You are not fully informed," Krestianov replied calmly, holding a glass of Georgian champagne. "You've been too busy with your festival. We have made great progress these past few weeks. The important thing is that I no longer work for someone else. I have no boss now. I work for myself. I work harder than ever, twenty hours a day. I know how to work. I don't like leveling, where somebody doing the same job good or bad gets the same pay. I think harder, and better quality work should be rewarded. That's perestroika. I am perestroika."

Krestianov had been the only man in his class at the hairdressing school in Omsk: "I've always been different. Since childhood, I was fired from four jobs. Only now with perestroika, people like me with minds of their own are needed. People who fired me are now begging me to come back. Last week the regional director of service industries asked me to be an adviser. He promised me a mountain of gold. I have so many ideas, there are so many possibilities. The train from Moscow takes two and a half days. On this train we will install our own beauty salon. The women can use our services and save time."

"Lies, lies," Belichenko interrupted. "There's nothing, nothing. Only debts."

"We have calculated everything," Krestianov insisted. "The person who replaced Dr. Zaslavsky as director of the Institute of Economics is our adviser. That person has also invested in our cooperative. Our bankers are very sympathetic. Our consultant verifies that we can make a profit."

"Stop!" Belichenko bellowed.

"But your jazz festival was once only a dream," Krestianov said. "Today's dream is tomorrow's reality."

"They are dreams," Belichenko insisted: "Only dreams."

Pop music was just terrible in the sixties. I really hated Cream and the Rolling Stones and the way they made the blues so boring. Stupid hippies playing dumb music. Everything got distorted and out of shape. I made my first LP in the seventies. Talk about your classic American success story. The kid comes through the door. Everybody was saying: "Yeah, man, you're the greatest." Phony people falling all over you. Cigar smoking fat cats telling you how big you're going to be—pulling out those little brown bottles. Soon it's all blowing your head wide open. When I started to do smack, right away I knew it was for me. I could hide in there.
—Willy (Mink) DeVille

7

CHET BAKER
HOW ABOUT A SNIFFETTE?

IF YOU HAVE TO EARN A LIVING, BOY, AND THE PRICE
THEY MAKE YOU PAY IS LOYALTY, BE A DOUBLE AGENT—
AND NEVER LET EITHER OF THE TWO SIDES KNOW YOUR
REAL NAME.

—GRAHAM GREENE

In the dirty old years, the name was Staccato, Johnny Staccato.

Staccato was born when John Vinocur said Mike could not use his own name writing for *Paris Passion*, an English-language monthly with miniscule circulation. Concentrating on local social and cultural events, *Paris Passion* was far from being in competition with the mighty *International Herald Tribune*. To be denied the use of his own name was outrageous. An arbitrary use of power. They did not own his name. He had signed no exclusive contract with the *Trib*. No contract at all, as a matter of fact. He was a freelancer. Free. If he'd ever been hired, he would have quit.

Needing all the paychecks he could get, one misty day in the murky 1980s he went undercover for *Paris Passion*. Mike assumed the identity of the private investigator and jazz pianist played by John Cassavetes in the early black-and-white television cop show *Johnny Staccato*. Players like Ray Brown and Shelly Manne would be on camera. Mike was to become much too attached to the name. The P.I. would be called away from the keyboard by a damsel in distress, grab his gun from the hat-check girl, and race out the door. Cassavetes's costar in the series was his sidekick Waldo, the distinguished owner of the eponymous bar he worked in, played by Eduardo Ciannelli.

Mike's sidekick was a fuckup named Ricky Cheval. Cheval lived on Impasse de Minuit—Midnight Dead End—a cobbled path running a short way up the hill from Boulevard Clichy in Pigalle. Informed Parisians with money had been moving to Pigalle. Gentrified buildings with sprawling early-twentieth-century apartments suitable for large families ran down and up the hill from the fast food emporiums, pornographic showcases, and tourist traps on Boulevard Clichy. Taking kids to school, walking the dog, going shopping or to work, inhabitants were obliged to cross this honky-tonk high street. A string of hustlers tried to talk you inside the fleshpots for which they shilled—they grabbed your arm, followed you down the street. The quarter was considered safe because there were people on the streets day and night. Trouble was, the people were mostly the unemployed, hookers, drunks, white slavers, policemen bearing assault rifles, tourists from former Axis countries, and drug dealers. Safe from whom?

Impasse de Minuit was an oasis of cool and quiet in the midst of the Pigallian madness. Ricky Cheval presided over what he fondly imagined to be an intellectual salon. People came and went speaking of Michelangelo, before throwing up. Money changed hands, but with discretion, and not all the time. Cheval liked to think that the people were there for the clever repartee more than the free lines of powders. It served as a dead-drop for under-deep-cover double agent Staccato.

Staccato was having a wake-up sniffette on Midnight Dead End one morning when Chet Baker appeared at the door. Chet was on his way from Paris to Amsterdam, and then to a gig in Brussels that same night. It was a long and geographically illogical haul. All Chet's roads led through Amsterdam, where he had a doctor. He had just stopped by Cheval's place to pick up enough fuel to get to the gas station. His Mercedes was idling in front, blocking the impasse. Cheval was proud to be the provider. Whoooosh! An entire gram went up Chet's nostrils in one full sweep. With a sly smile, skipping like a child who'd been caught with his nose in the candy jar, Chet took his leave.

Later that day, Cheval was bopping down Boulevard de Rochechouard looking like he had discovered a continent. It was the end of the twentieth century; there were no more continents to discover. Slinking in the opposite direction, Staccato was out of joint, over-tuned, looney-tooned—on a short leash. He would have liked to have felt more continental. Fortunately, Cheval's ship had come in. Or so he thought until it eventually became clear that it was in troubled waters. Right now, he had just the ticket for Staccato. "How about a sniffette?" he said.

As far as Johnny knew, Cheval had introduced the word *sniffette* into Franglais. It sounded so cute. Nothing harsh or dangerous like a snort or a shoot. We snort and shoot with rage, contempt, anger, aggression. We sniff a flower. We perceive with a sniff. Add the diminutive feminine French suffix and, voila—an adorable little sniffette.

Staccato's motto was moderation in all things. By that, however, he meant all things. He'd take only half a dose of just about anything, as long as it didn't come in a syringe. Staccato considered himself a reasonable junkie—talk about an oxymoron. If you had told him that his sniffettes were anything other than recreational, he would have considered you square. We are not talking about shiny white Girl. This was bad Boy. Downtown not Uptown. Skag, smack, junk, horse—*cheval* in French. In the sense that people come to resemble their names — a football coach named Winner; a dentist named Pullem; a rogue film director named Roeg; a French banker named Trichet (tricky) — Cheval was doomed from the start.

Doom was a good part of Chet Baker's charm. One day John Vinocur called from the paper to say that Chet had died in Amsterdam under mysterious circumstances. Would Johnny please go up there and sniff around? Talk about good casting. Please don't tell Vinocur.

Marking eras by some specific event or other is bound to be arbitrary. Still, it can be said that the myth of the bebop junkie, the image of jazz and drugs marching hand in hand, died along with Chet Baker when he fell out of a hotel window near the Zeedjik Bridge on Friday the thirteenth of May, 1988. There was a full moon. The French filmmaker Bertrand Fevre, who produced a documentary called *Chet's Romance*, first met Baker on another Friday the thirteenth when the moon was full. He did not consider that coincidental. Fevre's short documentary featured Baker singing and playing *I'm a Fool to Want You*. Twelve minutes long, shot in one day and short-listed in the short subject category of the Cannes Film Festival, Chet's rendition gives the impression that the song itself is the foolishly loved one.

Chet Baker lived in a land of foolish loves, Friday the thirteenths, full moons, one-day shoots, and last-minute selections. He was the Dostoyevsky of jazz — excess, anguish, and sorrow were his stuff. Undernourished, plaintive, lyrical, resourceful, enduring, endearing, he was his own worst enemy. After surfacing with Gerry Mulligan in the fifties, he began to sing and make his own records. His sound was warm and vulnerable. Much love has been made to Chet Baker records. He was compared to James Dean, his picture was in fashion magazines. As he proceeded to destroy himself, he discovered along the way that he was enjoying the destruction. His playing certainly improved—toward the end, on a good night, he could play jazz just about as well as it has ever been played. (There were not enough good nights.) Whatever else may have been destroyed, his love for heroin was never shaken.

Heroin was the perfect product. A capitalist's dream. A built-in bull market. Better than the armament business. There were no truces. The clientele was disposable but forever renewable. Cheval had stumbled upon the perfect supplier in a bar on the Rue de Lappe—a shitload of Polish brown sugar smuggled by sea in the wake of the fall of the Soviet Union by two alcoholic Latvian sailors who were not in a position to appreciate its true value. Knowing nobody in town and no better, on four days' leave from the port of Cherbourg, the Latvians made a deal with Cheval for twelve keys.

Conserving two grams a day for himself (reasonable, he figured), Cheval would unload the rest with great caution to a limited number of repeat customers at a fair price without cutting it with rat poison. Better figure three grams a day. Whatever—it would last forever, which he defined as three weeks. Cheval leapt on board with incredible lightness of being. He had been making a living playing cocktail piano in an American burger bar and grill in Les Halles called The Big One. When he was asked if he liked playing cocktail piano, he replied: "Depends on the cocktails." He did not yet realize it, but music was about to become a hobby.

With Chet, music always came first. He was one of the innovators who created the improvised American urban music that came to be called bebop. No revolutionary, he was not responsible for any dramatic musical breakthroughs, but his sound, certain turns of phrase, and where and how he placed notes have entered the vocabulary. His pianissimo touched you in a summertime place where the living is not easy. He was the last of them to remain faithful to heroin, long after the others had cleaned up or died young. The ability of that parched body and spirit to survive and even be nourished by the constant onslaught was some sort of a spooky affirmation. Europeans he had never met cried when he died.

Bebop's creators heard their articulation and phrases re-created uncredited on Hollywood soundtracks, and behind crooners. They played four sets a night for union scale in Mafia-controlled saloons, toured in broken-down vehicles, stayed in ratty hotels. Heroin was part of the huddle. It cured alienation for a minute, or seemed to. Today's young jazzmen wear three-piece suits, arrive on time, drink mineral water, and negotiate their own contracts. Heroin disappeared when a little respect arrived.

Cheval thought of himself as keeping the old tradition alive. Trying to play like Bud Powell, he liked to think he resembled Bill Evans. Marie-France's friend Brigitte thought he looked like Burt Lancaster. She was one of several young women who used to sit at the bar in The Big One, admiring Cheval. A responsible mother who loved her stage director husband, read *Le Monde*, listened to Mozart, and watched *Apostrophes,* Brigitte had been ready to take a lover. Nothing unusual there. Most married French women were ready. In all fairness, it went both ways. Taking a lover in Paris was up-front, on the surface, discussed in the cafés, one of life's necessary experiences. Marrieds who had been caught straying shrugged, and said to their partners: "Chérie, it's just a fuck. It's not so serious. Why don't you take a lover?" Brigitte was thinner than a high fashion model, with small breasts, long brown hair, shapely legs, and a damaged sense of reality. Flirting with heroin did not make her more realistic or zaftig. For years, it had remained a flirtation. Heroin can be a cheap way to go on vacation. Although Brigitte held a good straight job as an administrative assistant, she and her kinky husband went to orgies in private couples clubs on the Champs Élysées. She was a strange lady, and, a few weeks after she met Cheval, it was not a total surprise when Brigitte just up and moved in with him for the endless vacation on Midnight Dead End. The problem was that Brigitte was having more of an affair with cheval than Cheval.

With his new opportunity in a service industry with growth prospects, Cheval acknowledged that his ambition to write a symphony would have to be put on hold. He was happy enough to go on accompanying his chantoosies. The more zonked he was, the less like Bud Powell he sounded, and the more the girls liked it. Two waitresses at The Big One—a Swede and an Argentine—were wannabe singers with whom he made the rounds of flaky bars, pubs, and after-hours joints from Montparnasse to Montmartre. Accompanying singers was fun on horse. It was just demanding enough to keep him from nodding out, he enjoyed being around the girls, and it got Cheval out to meet new clients. If you did not know about his "personal problem," the way he slouched over the keyboard might have led you to think that he was—as Mike's mother used to call him, admiringly—"sickly sensitive."

Chet Baker was "such a sensitive musician," Madame Eglal Farhi said. With her effortless sophistication, referring to her as anything less than "Madame" would be somehow inappropriate. And don't call her before noon. "There was a sense of tragedy about him," she continued "Chet was sick, you know, he needed drugs. But he was our emblematic musician, our seal of authenticity. He was such a lonely, melancholy man. I was so fond of him." Madame Farhi's club, New Morning, was, along with the Village Vanguard, Yoshi's in Oakland, and Ronnie Scott's in London, a world-class venue. Such players as Branford and Wynton Marsalis, John Scofield, and Steve Swallow preferred to play several nights chez Madame Farhi than only one for the same money in a bigger, flashier venue with less karma. Appreciating late Chet Baker was mostly a European habit. Americans considered him "history." The New Morning was a home away from home for Chet toward the end when he didn't really have a home. Despite a reputation for showing up late, sick, or not at all, he could play the New Morning pretty much anytime he wanted—well past the time when his unreliability and drug-fueled aggression had alienated just about everybody else. "He was friendly, loyal, and warm," Madame Farhi said. "We always did good business with him. I think that one reason was because people wondered if each time would be the last."

"Sooner or later, something was bound to happen," Chet's Dutch road manager, Peter Huyts, said when he met Staccato at Schiphol Airport. "Everybody knew that." Huyts became worried when Chet did not show up for a radio broadcast in Laren. He was always late but he also always eventually showed up. It was Huyts who identified the body in the morgue. An autopsy ruled out physical violence. The hotel room door had been locked from the inside and drugs were found in it, which seemed to exclude foul play. The results of a blood test were not yet known, but it could be assumed that there were drugs in Chet Baker's blood. The police thought suicide a possibility. Huyts doubted it: "It was a hot night. He probably just nodded out one time too many, sitting on the windowsill. When I picked up his things later, his clothes were neatly folded in his suitcase. Somebody about to commit suicide doesn't do that."

Staccato checked into the same hotel. Obviously afraid of publicity, the owner refused to answer questions and to show him Chet's last room because it was "occupied." In his own room—one floor under Chet's, also in front—Staccato saw that only the transom opened. The central pane was permanently fixed. From the outside, all the windows looked alike, so how could anyone fall out? He wondered about that for a minute, but the police couldn't have overlooked something so obvious, and, besides, secret agent Staccato was under deep double-cover, in no condition to spend time with the police.

Baker had been embarrassed in the fifties when, a rising young star, he placed higher in the jazz polls than Clifford Brown and Dizzy Gillespie. He knew he wasn't in their league yet. He hated being considered a "great white hope." By the 1980s, great white hopes had gone out of style, along with pianissimos. His dire plight was also to a great degree his own fault—falling off a chair onstage is not a good career move. The creases on his face multiplied and deepened and his lips turned over the dentures he'd worn since his teeth were knocked out by a drug dealer in San Francisco. He began to resemble an old Indian, the last of a tribe that had seen a heap of suffering.

He'd learned Italian while doing a year in jail for drugs in Lucca. Eventually he became a sort of Italian folk hero, inspiring two generations of superior Italian trumpet players. Before a gig with the jazz pianist Romano Mussolini, he introduced himself to the dictator's son, and said: "Sure is a drag about your old man." Nobody's perfect. Moving around Europe three weeks here, two days there, wearing out welcomes, Chet would cut an album in a day for a thousand dollars. Just ask—anywhere, anytime. Cash only, please. Wim Wigt, who booked him in Europe and Japan, estimated that Chet was earning at least two hundred thousand dollars a year in the eighties. Wigt had a shaky reputation and his estimate was quite possibly low. Branford Marsalis talks about how shocked he was when he toured the Low Countries with Art Blakey as a young man and the legendary jazz giant and his entire band and its equipment were in one Volkswagen minibus. "Wigt wouldn't have done that to Sting," Branford said.

Belgian guitarist Philip Catherine, a reasonable fellow, described touring with Baker: "He was late a lot and there would be some very heavy panics. The pay wasn't always what it was supposed to be, or when, but the magic moments in the music made everything else worthwhile." Catherine's countryman the harmonica player Toots Thielemans toured Scandinavia with Chet. "There were long silences between tunes as decisions were made about what to play next," said Thielemans. Leading his own band, Toots always planned his sets in advance. He had an inventory of witty between-tune chatter. "Chet taught me a lot," he said. "He concentrated only on the music."

The German pianist Joachim Kuhn sat in with Chet at the New Morning a week before he died. He remembered thinking, "this can't go on much longer." Kuhn had found a house for Chet near his own in a quiet Parisian exurb. Baker had not lived in a house for a long time. He wanted to settle down, travel less, get higher fees, maybe take a few students. Kuhn was eight years old in the 1950s when he heard Baker for the first time in Berlin. He was very moved. He wanted to be a trumpet player for a while. It would have been nice for his old hero to live in his town.

Chet was tooling around the European Community in a new Alfa Romeo Giulia with Italian plates. Peter Huyts was often with him. "Chet was an expert driver; he would miraculously sober up behind the wheel," he said. The lanky, bespectacled Huyts looked too young to be a grandfather of two, and too straight to be a road manager of jazz bands. After losing his job as an electrical engineer, he had run a jazz club. Growing to love the music, he went out with Wim Wigt's clients like Gillespie and Blakey. Huyts figured he'd heard at least 150 Chet Baker concerts, and he probably knew him as well as anyone.

Despite the well-publicized Italian arrest, and Baker's having been deported, at one time or another, from Switzerland, West Germany, and Great Britain, there was never trouble crossing borders. "Not once," Huyts remembered. "It always puzzled me. Chet had a good 'act' for the *douane*. He knew how to play that game. He could turn on the charm. He was always losing things, and leaving things behind. But he took care of business when he had to. For many years, he used a mouthpiece Dizzy had given him. Took good care of it; made sure he never lost it. He was very proud of it, it had 'Birks' engraved on it." Gillespie got Chet his comeback gig in New York after the former white hope had learned to play with false teeth.

Staccato reached Dizzy on the phone at his home in New Jersey. "The major thing he lacked, you see," Dizzy said: "He was too tender. Jazz is a gutbucket thing. Great soloists have got to be able to get tough. He was too vulnerable."

A Dutch inactive addict who used to let Chet crash in his apartment remembered observing him search for an uncollapsed vein. There was one in his groin, but he kept missing it. Finally he found one in his neck. After the needle entered and the syringe emptied, his knees buckled, he held on to the sink and moaned: "Saline solution." The Dutch addict recognized an overdose and found the antidote. Some hours later, when Baker had recovered and was dressing to go to work, the Dutchman asked him: "Hey, man. Don't you ever get tired of this number?"

"Yeah, I hate the road," Chet said: "Hotels, airports, getting guys for gigs."

"No," the Dutchman said. "I mean shooting dope."

"Oh, that. I never think about that."

Back in Paris, one more cover-confirming front-page credit under his belt, Staccato was ordered immediately out again by his secret minder. This time he would play a trombone rather than take notes. His handlers were embedding him with a jazz trio that was being sent by the cultural attaché to play a one-nighter in Algiers. What they really wanted was a top-secret rundown on North African drug networks. A routine assignment.

Brushing up on his arpeggios, scales, show tunes, and Arabic, Staccato hired bassist Mort Bradley and the drummer Haynes McBee. Mort was very pale, he did not see much sun. Haynes was robust, smart, and about as black and good-natured as a human being can be. Cheval said they could rehearse in his place on Impasse de Minuit. Between tunes, watching Cheval so majestically whacked in his place, Staccato thought, thank goodness *he* wasn't that bad. Johnny Staccato was only a role, after all—he could step out of it anytime he wanted.

When the rehearsal was over, Cheval said Haynes could leave his drums overnight. Haynes pointed out that he'd have to pick them up at five to make the early flight to Algiers. Was Cheval sure he would be there to open the door? Cheval said he never went to bed before noon.

The next morning, Staccato and Bradley were waiting at the departure gate in Orly at dawn with what turned out to be unjustified calm. Because all was not well on Midnight Dead End. Haynes arrived at five, rang the bell, waited, rang again, knocked, and knocked again. He climbed up a tree to a window and knocked on that. No sign of life. Climbing a tree on a residential street in Pigalle at five o'clock in the morning is not recommended for black people. He worried that Cheval may have nodded terminally out. Haynes went down and found a pay phone on the boulevard and called. No answer. He returned and poked around some more. Not even a mouse stirred on the Impasse de Minuit. He went back down and called again, and this time a strange voice answered. The voice said that Cheval was snoring on the floor but Haynes was welcome to pick up his drums anyway.

The weight of the drums was meant to be averaged over all three tickets—the excess would be astronomical on any one of them. When boarding at Orly was announced at six forty-five, Haynes still not there, Mort and Johnny decided to leave anyway. The Air Algeria agent said there was another flight at three; Haynes could come on that one. Staccato knew that the drummer would not have the cash to pay for all the excess weight, but the Air Algeria guy said that he would probably still be on duty and that he could do the necessary spreading. Against all odds, the weight was spread, Haynes arrived, and Staccato did not have to play in a trombone-bass duo, which would have been a bit too undercover for comfort.

When he got back to Paris, Staccato yelled at Cheval for his fuck-up. A fat two-and-two took the edge off, and anyone could see that Cheval was, to put it mildly, distracted. He had rented a safe deposit box in a bank called BRED. He loved having a stash in a bank called BRED. As his daily doses increased and his inventory shrank, Cheval began to step harder on the remainder. He peddled it retail in the clubs on Rue Oberkampf, not cool. Cheval was visiting the BRED vault more and more often and the retired Legionnaire in charge of it grew suspicious. After finding powder traces on Cheval's blotter, the guard, who had served in Vietnam, called *les stupes.*

The French narcs who arrived one morning during wake-up-sniffette hour on Midnight Dead End had not been alerted to Johnny's deep double-cover, and under no circumstances could they be told about it. Staccato had a hard time talking his way out of that one. He was saved by a notarized copy of his contract with an Interpol-controlled offshore publisher to write a book about hard drugs in contemporary Francophone culture.

Have I ever lied to you?

You could change anything in Argentina—religion, the law, the money, twenty thousand presidents. Just don't change the tango. Ask them who Bach, Picasso, or John Coltrane was and they don't know. Once, when Aaron Copland came to hear us, I said, "Play good, you guys. Aaron Copland is out there." They said, "Who's Aaron Copland?" That's the world of the tango for you—drinking, drugs, prostitutes, cops, gigolos, thieves. Idiots. I got out of that business. I hated it. I found another way.
—Astor Piazzolla

8

BOB DYLAN

DR. PITRE'S NOMINAL APHASIA

DUPONT: "WE ARE WHAT WE REMEMBER."
SIMON JORDAN: "PERHAPS WE ARE ALSO—
PREPONDERANTLY—WHAT WE FORGET."

—MARGARET ATWOOD, *ALIAS GRACE*

Mike was having a hard time remembering the name of that folk singer who wrote "It's Alright, Ma (I'm Only Bleeding)." He'd been forgetting names lately. It did not worry him because he'd been led to understand that forgetting familiar names is not necessarily Alzheimer's, but a friendlier affliction the French call, after the doctor who discovered it, *aphasie nominale de Pitre* (Dr. Pitre's nominal aphasia).

He considered forgetting so many names to be an ethical failure. A failure of social will, if you will. A failure on a human level. Underneath it all, what Mike was really saying was: "You see, my friend, you are not important enough for me to take the trouble to remember your name." At best, it was embarrassing.

Forgetting faces is different. He did that too. Forgetting a face might be the face's fault. Age can change a face beyond recognition. Names and faces of women he had successfully courted escaped him. With hindsight, he did not take enough responsibility for his own seductions. Basically, like most men, he took what came his way. He looked back more in sorrow than guilt. His stance had been: "I'll be the best lover I can, but if you don't have an orgasm that's your problem." He would really try, you understand, but in the end they either came or they didn't, and he wasn't going to feel guilty about not being guilty about it. The fact remained that he had not been thoughtful. He did not think to buy flowers. Birthdays passed forgotten. To be fair, on his end, no hoot was given about forgotten birthdays. The majority were women who took such things seriously—nubile New York girls, no more or less insecure, beautiful, or intelligent than the rest. They deserved better. He remembered only eyes here, breasts there, some asses perhaps, an armpit or two. He forgot entire relationships. One night while he was visiting Marcel, by then a musician living in Brooklyn, Mike went along to one of his gigs in the West Village. They arrived at the same time as the band working in the basement bar next door; everybody was saying hello on the sidewalk. A woman of a certain age who was a pianist accompanying the other group's singer introduced herself to Marcel. Hearing his name, she asked him: "Are you related to Michael?" He pointed to Mike on the curb. She did a double take, looked at him sideways, and said: "You don't remember me, do you?" What a terrible thing to hear from a woman. Had they made love? Maybe she'd had his child and he'd never known. What *was* her name?

Forgetfulness is a particularly serious problem for expatriates who have to remember deadlines, and know something about the rules and regulations of two different bureaucracies. Renew your French residence card in June. Your American passport expires in January. February is *carte de presse* month. French and American income tax deadlines are three months apart. The upmarket accountant Mike's marginal lifestyle required was licensed in both countries, and he cost more than the taxes. Remembering to do it all was memory-challenging, nerve-wracking, panic-inducing, and expensive. You buy off bureaucracies with your income tax like buying protection from the Mafia. You pay to keep the system away. In Mike's case, two systems. Three if you count the European Union. Although hanging between different computer networks in competing languages with often incompatible software also has its advantages.

Thank goodness. Mike's nominal aphasia just split. The name of the folk singer he couldn't remember was Bob Dylan. Bet you knew that all the time.

A Bob Dylan review, from 1978:

Bob Dylan's first of four concerts at the Bercy Omnisport Arena in Paris last night was more a miracle than a concert. It is easy to get carried away and exaggerate the importance of such hyperstar events, but when 7,000 people are lifted off the ground by an invisible force, it can be called miraculous.

You go to a Dylan concert these days thinking . . . Oh well, just the same old intelligent songs again. But they turned out to be not at all the same. They were more. He is exploring the subtleties of his own material.

Published sheet music of popular tunes provides only the barest harmonic outlines. Only four chords may be indicated for an entire song, where actually 14 are required. Dylan once accompanied himself like that . . . clang clang clang clang. Only four chords, the same ones, mostly in the same key. They would work anyway because of the poetry, and because he has always been somehow miraculous.

It is as if he is only now completing the songs. Far from having become tired, they are refreshed, refurbished. He approaches them as a musician not an ego-tripper. He does not posture on stage. If you did not know it was Dylan up there, you might think he was the lead singer with somebody else's band.

His current band is tight, spirited, swinging. Like it was put together by Motown. Plenty of percussion, heavy guitars, boosted basslines, a saxophone, a violin and a backing chorus of three Supreme-like women wearing white gowns. They did "Blowin' in the Wind" as a hymn, a choir of angels humming behind the preacher. He crooned "I Want You" like a '50s torch singer. "Ballad of a Thin Man" became a down-home blues. "It's Alright Ma (I'm Only Bleeding)" could almost have been James Brown. "Just Like a Woman" sounded like a spiritual, "All I Really Want to Do" like a marching band, and "All Along the Watchtower" had more to do with the Jimi Hendrix version than his own.

This tour's production is so visually slick that some critics have complained about it being "too Las Vegassy." But Dylan has always been ahead of the critics. When they finally got used to his out-of-tune folksy twang, he electrified. He was booed. He stopped protesting and sang love songs. He turned to country and western before it became a fad. He was booed. Now that it is a fad, he had not one C&W song on the program. His last time in Paris, 1966, during the Vietnam War, he hung this enormous American flag behind him on the stage of the Olympia Theater, just to stay ahead of us. He was booed.

Tomorrow is Dylan's final concert in Bercy.

Talk about a puff job. Mike had had to fight off an urge to spike it. The day the review ran, his telephone rang and an out-of-the-blue voice said: "Wanna hear the news from the mountaintop?" The voice turned out to be Dylan's press officer, a star in his own right. What was his name? He was a friend of Mike's. "The news from the mountaintop is that it's good to know that there is at least one critic with good ears." Now, the man on top of the mountain would say that, wouldn't he? The notice was what might be called a rave. Thinking back, Mike wondered if he really liked it that much. Critics should never write about music listened to after smoking a joint. It's like being stoned in a supermarket—you will like what you liked to begin with but a whole lot more.

As a reward, Dylan's press guy biked over two all-access passes for the final Parisian concert, and Mike invited a young female journalist he'd been thinking of wooing. An all-access pass to a Bob Dylan concert was a good woo tool. They were both writing for an alternative weekly paper formed after a journalist named Tom Moore wrote an article for *Life* magazine about a bank robber in Brooklyn who was looking to finance his friend's sex-change operation. Selling the rights for what was to become the movie *Dog Day Afternoon,* Moore and his partners started an English-language magazine named the *Paris Métro.* People called it the *Village Voice* of Paris. Writers wrote what they wanted the way they wanted for very little money. The perfect place for Mike. Once more, he was not permitted to use his real name. As with *Paris Passion,* the *International Herald Tribune,* a daily newspaper, said that the local weekly the *Paris Métro* was competition. In the *Paris Métro,* Mike wrote under the name of . . .

Bingo. Dylan's press guy's name was Paul Wasserman.

The French call a woman whose name they cannot remember *Machine.* Wasserman came over to greet Mike and Machine in the press seats. "The man from the top of the mountain wants to meet you," he said. My goodness. What was there to say to Bob Dylan:

"You're my hero? You changed my life? Can I have your autograph for my sister?"

"I don't like going backstage," Mike mumbled. Machine kicked him in the shins and hissed in his ear: "I want to meet Bob Dylan." She was right. Mike was chicken. Fear was for the birds. Valor was the better part of caution. Mike and Machine marched with their all-access passes through a succession of security checkpoints, and were finally ushered into a storeroom lit by a bare, dusty hanging lightbulb. The atmosphere was not unlike that of the room in the dumpy hotel near Gare de L'Ést in which he'd once interviewed a visitor from Saturn named Sun Ra. That room had been haunted by the ghosts of lonely sailors. This one was haunted by alienated rockers.

In a sweaty white T-shirt and baggy jeans, Dylan was, like his bodyguard, sipping from a beer can. Cases of beer were stacked along the wall. The ceiling was peeling. Dylan's face was in the shadows, backlit by the bare bulb. And he had been backlit onstage all evening as well. No eyes to be seen. Machine looked faint. Mike was short of breath. As they often do, Dylan's lyrics went through his mind: "Life sometimes must get lonely."

Dylan looked like a World War was passing through his brain. There was nobody there to call his bluff. "Okay, I've had enough," he seemed to be thinking: "What else can you show me?"

To break the ice, Mike handed him a copy of the *Paris Métro*. The bodyguard said he'd heard about it, and it was supposed to be good. Dylan said he'd look forward to reading it. Mike recalled Dylan's line "You shouldn't let other people get your kicks for you."

That was about it. Not much else happened. There were awkward silences. Being no Lester Bangs, Mike did not split with Bobby to hang out and get smashed. They did not sit in Dylan's crib and listen to music together until dawn. Having shaken Dylan's hand, Machine said she'd never wash hers again. Machine had beautiful hands. Mike imagined Machine telling her grandchildren about meeting Bob Dylan.

"Who's Bob Dylan?" the kids would probably ask.

Mike saw Dylan again some years later, performing on a large stage in a dale of a hilly lawn in the leafy Parc de Sceaux, just outside Paris. It was still daylight when the concert began. At first the music was shaky, and without much conviction. During an instrumental interlude that featured a guitar solo by Mick Taylor, Dylan went behind the stage to woodshed something with his guitar. When he returned, the performance began to coalesce, it quickly picked up speed, and there were enthusiastic ovations.

The following afternoon, Mike arrived ten minutes early at the almost empty Brasserie Lorraine on Place des Ternes, where an interview was scheduled. Inserting fresh batteries in his cassette machine, he looked up and suddenly, sitting down at his table, there was Bob Dylan. He'd appeared on time, out of nowhere, with no entourage in sight. Just pale, underfed, uncombed, bowlegged Bob Zimmerman, wearing shades.

Dylan had played some of his old hits in Parc de Sceaux, and Mike asked if that didn't get boring.

"I don't understand this 'hits' business," Dylan said. "It's like doing Shakespeare or something. The lines are good. I *want* to sing them." Later, Mike checked the tape. Yes, it was there, all right. But to write that Bob Dylan had compared himself to Shakespeare might be a cheap shot. Still, he said it. It might even be true.

As a born-again Christian, did he still stand by his earlier songs?

"You mean, 'It's easy to see without looking very far that not much is really sacred'? Yeah, I still stand by that. It's like it was just written yesterday. 'Flesh-colored Christs that glow in the dark.' I find that all still pretty much true."

The rock press had reported that he had remained Hasidic after becoming a born-again Christian. "He lives on another planet," Joan Baez told the newspaper *Le Monde*. Formerly part of the Parc de Sceaux tour, Baez went her own way just before Paris. She explained that she had thought she would sing with him, not be his opening act. There had been a series of humiliations, fights, and compromises. No hard feelings, she said: "I spent one wonderful day with him. He was very funny. If he was more of this world he certainly would have helped me."

It was said that when Baez told him she was leaving the tour, he ran his hand up those once-familiar thighs and asked her where she'd got them new muscles. He was not taking her quite seriously. She had been famously in love with him. He famously mistreated her. It may sound far-fetched, and it's certainly not objective, but perhaps one reason for playing with her head like that was because, deep down, he did not like the way she sang his songs.

Dylan was as much from another time as from another planet, and Mike asked him what other period of history would he like to have been born in.

"We played this coliseum in Verona," the poet replied: "And at the foot of the stage there was a huge pit. Somebody told me that was where the blind poets used to read before they got drowned. Something like that. I probably came along at just about the right time."

What about being born in a different place?

"You mean what if I'd been born black or something? Maybe I'd have had more to say, maybe less. Maybe I wouldn't have bothered at all. Some people are in a position where they are just unable to express their feelings. People look at you and think you are so-and-so, but that is not really who you are."

Mike asked if the opportunity to write gospel songs on the piano instead of folk music on a guitar might be one reason he decided to be born-again.

"Not exactly," the songwriter laughed. He did not say no: "These periods of time go by so quickly it's hard to remember. But I did stumble on some new chordal structures, and other possibilities, which surprised me as much as anybody. My focus starts to disintegrate fairly quickly. I can't stay too long with one thing."

"He not busy being born is busy dying," he'd famously written. Miles Davis expressed something similar when he said: "I have to keep changing, it's like a curse." Miles and Dylan had a lot in common. Fans resented them both after they successfully combined their tradition with rock. Both created new traditions. They each had a reputation as being acerbic, inaccessible, and prone to bad humor. They were famous for knowing how to disappear. A backlit Dylan is not unlike Miles with his back to the audience. And both of them had staying power and continued to perform on more or less endless tours into their sixties.

"Some critic once compared my band to Bruce Springsteen," Dylan complained, "because we both had saxophone players, or something. Sometimes they called it disco. I don't know why, maybe it's something I've done, but the press just doesn't seem to know who I am. They just take the heart out of me."

"No man sees my face and lives," he had written. Dylan's backlit face in Bercy had reminded Mike of a terrorist keeping his features in the shadows to avoid recognition on camera. The sound mix had drowned out his words, and it was as though his lyrics were backlit too. The audience could neither hear nor see him, and he was not about to shout any louder or look any of them in the eye. You might wonder why a singing poet who goes to the considerable investment and bother of a major world tour would hide his face and his words from his audience.

Critics had been writing that he was "tired," and "bored" onstage. "Shadowy" would have been a better word. It may have been insecurity. There must have been times when he asked himself how come he writes this far-out shit. Does anybody understand it? He probably didn't understand himself half the time. "To draw a crowd with my guitar," he told a journalist: "That's about the most heroic thing I can do."

Waiters began to set tables for dinner in Brasserie Lorraine as Mike said that Dylan's song "Neighborhood Bully" was being called a "Zionist statement." What did he have to say?

"People say I'm political," he answered. "But I have no input into that. Politics is just some thing they throw to people, like a bone. It changes nothing. To keep things in order, people seem to need something to distrust. If you're not mistrusting somebody, everything would be too cool."

Was he saying that an honest politician would lie and cheat on purpose because he knows people need something to distrust? Are some crooked politicians in fact people only playing at being bad for the public good? That would make a good Bob Dylan song.

Did he ever wake up with anguish in the middle of the night?

"No, I don't wake up, because I can't go to sleep in the first place. You don't realize how valuable peace is until you've lost it." He took a breath, and continued: "The thing is, the person who's creating the stuff never knows what he's doing. I never ask myself why I do it. It's what I do, that's all. And I think I'm just getting good at it."

Beginning to pack up, Mike asked: "Do you ever worry about repeating yourself?"

"I don't know who I am anyway from one day to another," he shrugged. "So I don't know what there is to repeat."

The check had been paid. Which was odd because no Bob Dylan people had been visible during the entire interview. Trying to figure it out, Mike almost forgot to ask: "What were you practicing behind the bandstand yesterday?"

"Oh that?" Dylan laughed: "Just trying to remember the words to 'Mr. Tambourine Man.'"

Barbershops & Whorehouses VIII

When Don Henley said that he did not consider rock to be an art form, Mike asked him: "What is art?"

"Neil Young had a dog named Art," Henley replied. "He wrote a song for him, 'For Art's Sake.' Art is Neil Young's dog."

9

DON BUDGE
PLAYING WITH WANDS

THERE IS NO CONTRADICTION IN THINGS, ONLY IN
THE WORDS WE INVENT TO REFER TO THINGS. IT IS THE
WORD "I" WHICH IS ARBITRARY AND WHICH CONTAINS
WITHIN IT ITS OWN INADEQUACY AND ITS OWN
CONTRADICTION.

—ALEXANDER TROCCHI, *YOUNG ADAM*

You can walk for hours in Paris without seeing anything seriously ugly. French public transport is reliable; the health care system basically works. There's a thirty-five hour work week, and six or seven weeks' paid vacation a year. Things are so good in the culture business that even freelance actors and musicians go on strike. When a holiday falls on a Tuesday or a Thursday, it is often connected to the nearest weekend. These are called *ponts,* bridges. The ease with which the French build these bridges is one example of how they have resolved the quality of life equation in favor of life. They accept lost productivity in exchange for more quality time. All in all, they work some three hundred hours a year less than Americans. Not to imply they do not work hard. Hour for hour they are more productive than Americans. The French are well educated and, given half an incentive, industrious. They have built, despite many faults, a fine social system with a sophisticated and well-maintained infrastructure. Not to sound condescending. Of course they are sophisticated—we all know that. It's just that they decided that being a rich country was enough. The physical and psychic price that Americans pay to keep getting richer and richer all the time is too high for them. Whether they can continue to get away with that is another matter. Determining where they draw the line between rich and too rich would go a long way toward figuring out the French.

The French have a love affair with anarchy. They'll admit it; they adore disorder. They go on strike as often as possible, sometimes just for the fun of it. When strikes are too frequent, widespread, or violent, their solid infrastructure can get shaky. Mike went to a Frank Zappa concert not long after he arrived in France. The hall was invaded by students demanding free music for the people. They climbed onstage and the music ground to a halt. People were screaming and making fists. Marie-France clapped her hands in glee, jumped up and down, and shouted: *"Quel bordel!"* What a mess! Zappa was not amused.

It is a bit surprising that the French can be so successful at stuff like building airplanes and railroads. You tend to think of them more in connection with making cheese, wine, and love—and surrendering—but France hums right along. Paris is a first-class city to live in—as long as you are white, not poor, reasonably well connected, and *sortable*. In other words, like almost everywhere else, but better. Garbage is collected, the buildings are constantly being resurfaced, there is nightlife downtown. French trains are clean, quiet, swift, comfortable, economical, and (when not on strike) reliable. Getting from one European city to another by fast train is a big part of that inch of difference between France and America. No early check-ins, security hassles, no buckling seatbelts, waiting for luggage, and, most of all, no leaving the ground.

Any country where Coca-Cola is more expensive than wine cannot be all bad. French advertising, however, sucks as much as anyplace else, that inch notwithstanding. They will not stop movies for commercials, that is just not done (but you'd better duck before and after.) Edited reruns of NFL games have no commercials. Better yet, they cut out boring scrimmages. Changeovers in tennis matches do not necessarily include sponsored messages (between sets, though, be warned). While the players exchanged sides, you often see absolutely nothing happen. It is glorious. Dead air. Sometimes it's even better than the matches, especially when they're filled with double-faults and unforced errors. The camera pans on youngsters picking their noses, players munching bananas, teenagers waving, coaches looking worried, senior citizens looking folkloric, pretty young girls being young and pretty. Patrick Rafter's girlfriend looking healthy and wealthy . . . Pete Sampras's wife . . . Tim Henman's . . . Andy Roddick's girlfriend . . .

Mute a tennis match on television and listen to a Count Basie record—you'd be surprised how often they are in sync. There are other things in common. You play not work both jazz and tennis, and there are sets in each. They both involve real-time risks, instinct is essential, both require concentration and consistency, and you have to find your own rhythm in each discipline. Those long baseline rallies when the players are just trying to keep the ball in play recall a jazz soloist running his scales and warhorse licks to get revved up. Lose your groove in the middle of either kind of set and it takes unusual motivation, confidence, and endurance to come back—and body language is essential.

When Mike was in the steel business, he was a Wednesday night tennis hacker on stock-broker-priced courts in a geodesic dome in the Borough of Queens. During business hours, he would think about base and bass lines, about "Topsy" and topspin, and about

the nature of swing. He was thinking about the existential implications of the parallels between tennis and jazz when he should
have been thinking about cash flow. Not thinking about money
was hard work. He liked money as much as anybody—he just did
not like to think about it. Most of all, he did not want to think
about it in the office. He'd sit in at clubs and sleep little, then
take power breakfasts at the Algonquin. Weekends, he would sit at
home and practice long tones while watching baseball. There were
Monday night gigs with the painter Larry Rivers in a band called
the Upper Bohemia Six at the Five Spot Cafe. Both of them had
other things to think about. Mike felt right at home. When he improvised, sometimes he worried about Dome Steel instead of concentrating on chord changes. He was, you might say, of split mind.
When he improvised poorly, or lost at tennis—one tended to lead
to the other—it added up to a self-serving prophecy. He was leading Dome Steel down the road to bankruptcy. His whole life was
going into the red.

Bankruptcy can be avoided, or at least delayed, by never staying in any one endeavor long enough to make a profit. During his
international music critic period in Paris, Mike went to hear Michel
Petrucciani and Jim Hall play a duo concert. He knew the little
crippled pianist Petrucciani from the French California, and Hall
was the favorite guitar player of a lot of people who could not agree
on much else. After the concert, the musicians and an entourage
went to the corner brasserie for a late dinner. Fifteen of them were
sitting at four pushed-together tables. Before ordering, a student
asked the waiter to make sure there would be separate checks. Hall
turned to ask Mike: "Do they take American Express here?"

A cake had been ordered by Petrucciani; it would be Hall's birthday at midnight. As people began to whisper *"gâteau,"* Hall got up
and went off supposedly in search of the men's room. A friend

spotted him slinking out the street door just as the waiter arrived with the cake. He rushed out in pursuit, and, returning, the friend explained: "Jim went to his hotel. He said thanks a lot for everything, but he couldn't handle the cake, and everybody wishing him happy birthday, and figuring out fifteen separate checks. He paid the whole bill with his American Express card."

The thinking man's guitarist, Hall thought a lot of his peers were taking less risks as they got older, but he knew Picasso and Stravinsky had not given up like that, and, during dinner, he'd told Mike that he wanted "to go out like they did." He also recommended interviewing the tennis legend Donald Budge—"you'll never meet a more enthusiastic jazz fan"—who was coming to Paris soon for the French Open.

Mike met Budge on a clear June day in front of the cute four-star hotel on Île St. Louis where Budge always stayed in Paris. He seemed happy, and at home. He'd won the French Open, in 1939. There was a statue of him in the Roland Garros tennis compound. Today's players take the ball early on the rise, and hit it harder. Budge started all that—"I knew I was on to something"—when he built his style on "a combination of Ellsworth Vines's power, and taking the ball early like Fred Perry. It seemed so innovative at the time."

Mike asked Budge which tennisman played most like a jazz musician.

"Gee, I never thought about that," Budge replied. He stroked his jaw: "I guess Charlie Parker played like he was hitting a rising ball. The cats must have spent a lot of time trying to figure that one out."

Tommy Dorsey once promised Budge he could play drums with his band if he defeated Vines in an exhibition in Madison Square Garden. When victor Budge entered the ballroom of the Hotel New Yorker that evening, Dorsey motioned drummer Dave Tough away, and Budge sat in his place. A dancer requested Dorsey's hit "Marie," but the leader replied: "You'll have to talk to the drummer. It's his band."

Recently, a panel of experts somewhere voted "flatulent" and "jazz" two of the ten ugliest words in the English language. If, however, an activity can be rated according to the people who admire it, Donald Budge made jazz smell good, and he had very good ears. His peers, the tennis elite, hung out with rich WASP power brokers— executives, bankers, lawyers, politicians—and they wore suits and ties and made million-dollar deals in segregated country clubs. Not the kind of people who got excited about improvisation, either in music or life. They did not welcome the unexpected. To remain one of their number while going out of his way to relate to the musicians took exceptional intelligence and mobility.

"You can learn a lot when you listen to what the good players have to say," Budge said. Mike assumed he meant both jazz and tennis players, unconsciously underscoring the connection he was attempting to make. Why was this stupid jazz and tennis theory so important to him? Budge was one of the few people who could explain it. He was not stuck in a box, or in the past. Passionate about the best in the music, Budge was also tolerant of its flaws. His educated instinct allowed him to not automatically dislike music that did not touch him personally. He kept asking for explanations— about Miles playing rock, for example—and he weighed pros and cons while listening to the answers.

Recalling the many musicians he had met, he repeated how honored he was to have known them. The bandleader Artie Shaw once took him to hear "a guy who is going to set the world on fire. It was Lester Young with Count Basie. Artie said, 'It's what Lester doesn't play that's the most interesting.'" Budge told a Lester Young story: "He was playing in a club in Cleveland while I was playing in a tournament there, and I went to hear him. I applauded after he played the melody of 'Body And Soul'—before he even started to improvise. The melody had never sounded so beautiful to me. Later, Lester came over to me and said: 'Nobody ever did that before. Thank you very much.' He loved to play melodies."

After listening to an up-tempo recording by his pal Benny Goodman, Budge went out and won a match, the music still in his head. Just pronouncing the names—Clifford Brown, Phil Woods, Ray Brown, Shelly Manne—gave him pleasure. He called Bill Evans "my pin-up." They had met when the pianist introduced himself after a set in the Village Vanguard. "Mr. Budge," he said. "I heard you were a jazz fan. I've been watching you all night. You sure know how to listen to music." The next night, he asked to borrow twenty dollars. Budge gave it to him and asked if it would be enough. Evans said that would do it.

"It's so sad," Budge said. "What was he on? Heroin? Never having taken drugs, I don't understand it. What a waste. I cried when he died. Do you know his rendition of "A Child is Born"? It's so moving. To think there will be no more Bill Evans recordings."

Then he exclaimed: "Oh, I've got it." The answer to the question about the connection between the athletes and the musicians: "Probably John McEnroe was the tennis player most like a jazz musician. He had that instinct you cannot learn. He was not a great disciplinarian, he didn't sweat practicing and working out like Borg or Lendl. It was as though he played tennis with a wand rather than a racket. Bill Evans played the piano with a wand."

I try never to go to the same restaurant twice. Or if I do, I always order something different. If I have appointments in the same place several days in a row, I take different routes getting there. If I give two concerts in the same hall, I make sure to repeat absolutely nothing.
—*Bobby McFerrin, improviser*

10

STEPPENWOLF
BRILLIANT ECCENTRICS

*BECAUSE JOSEF'S MEMORY WAS MALEVOLENT AND
PROVIDED HIM WITH NOTHING TO MAKE HIM CHERISH
HIS LIFE IN HIS COUNTRY, HE CROSSED THE BORDER
WITH A BRISK STEP AND NO REGRETS.*
—MILAN KUNDERA, *IGNORANCE*

"It's not every day you get to say, 'I have a movie opening on the Champs Élysées today,'" Fred Haines said, lifting his eyes toward heaven.

Haines had studied Gaelic and read the book three times before writing an Oscar-nominated screenplay for Joe Strick's movie of James Joyce's *Ulysses*. Later, Fred learned German so he could read Hermann Hesse in the original to write a scenario for, and direct, *Steppenwolf.*

Lack of concentration was not one of Haines's problems. He could sit so still and concentrate so hard on erudite material over such extended periods of time that his producer, Hamburger, nicknamed him "Fly Face," after the Dick Tracy character. Hamburger's "Gee whiz! I'm a Hollywood producer" number totally baffled Marie-France, who needed subtitles under his hipster stance and Brooklyn accent. Was he being serious when he said, "A movie without Marlon Brando is not a movie"? And what did such New World alienation as "Switzerland is the Beverly Hills of Europe" really mean? Mike reminded her that Louis Armstrong had told somebody who asked him what jazz was: "Man, if you gotta ask you'll never know."

There were intellectuals on both sides of the Atlantic who felt that Hamburger represented the brilliant, eccentric, energetic, creative side of America. If only Americans could be more like Hamburger. Over the years, his ironic, inside-out, post-Brucian antics have moved into the Hollywood mainstream. Such stoned mindsets were later explored by Robert Altman *(The Player),* Milos Forman *(Man on the Moon),* Spike Jonze *(Being John Malkovich),* and others. Not to say that Altman or Forman or Jonze was influenced by Hamburger—they probably never heard of him.

Hamburger's act was more an endless succession of licks than a complete number. A lick cannot be copyrighted. Irony cannot be patented. Hamburger was in the public domain. When he said the holes in your Swiss cheese are somebody else's Swiss cheese, it was clear that he was talking directly to Mike. It meant, don't worry about what journalists call hard news—make your own news. Don't let other people get their kicks for you. Hamburger named Mike "Off-Season Charlie." He said: "What I like most about you is you have absolutely no ambition."

Off-Season Charlie really knew how to disappear. He was an adept explorer of holes in Swiss cheese. Although it was not that simple. Mike had plenty of ambition, just not for power or money. "Money is a sign of reality," Hamburger liked to say. "If somebody offers you money for what you do then you are living in the real world." He consciously avoided reality. He preferred to lay back in the hole and let the cheese come to him. The way his mind worked, Hamburger reminded Mike of Stanley Kubrick. Both assimilated an immense amount of information, much of it useless. Uselessness was a big part of their talent—the sum total was meant to overflow. Kubrick was able to channel it all. In a way, Hamburger was a failed Kubrick—a would-be Kubrick, a mere brilliant eccentric. The expression "brilliant eccentric" implies the prefix "nothing more than a . . ." Hamburger was content to be a brilliant eccentric. Being brilliantly eccentric was more important to him than being, say, a filmmaker. Accused of being "out of line" by a haughty maître d' in a restaurant in Lausanne, Hamburger replied: "Yes, yes. That's exactly where I want to be: out of line."

Having spent some years living in what he described as the "only chicken coop in Beverly Hills," Hamburger was the perfect choice to produce a documentary called *Mondo Hollywood.* The credit led nowhere. His career was not moving forward. Those who knew him were convinced it never would. But for Hamburger, not getting anywhere could be made an achievement in itself. Not getting his act together was the whole point. Not getting it together was his act. It was more or less taken for granted that preproduction was all there would ever be to the making the Hamburger-produced movie of *Steppenwolf.*

The encore surprised Hamburger as much as anybody. It had taken three years of living "on the arm," as he called being on-the-cuff to-the-max, in Basel to coax Herman Hesse's heirs into giving him an option on the rights. The writer had expressly forbidden a movie of *Steppenwolf* in his will. Pulling it off was a world-class hustle. Since it cost rather than earned money, Hamburger's joy was unqualified. He wooed dentists from Bel Air into transferring cash to Switzerland from under their mattresses for preproduction money. Fred Haines's *Ulysses* credit helped. Investing in an art film of a German literary classic to be directed in Switzerland by the American writer of an Academy Award-nominated adaptation of James Joyce was a classy way to go offshore.

Hamburger hosted a party for friends and investors one sodden late autumn afternoon in a borrowed Alpine lodge in the canton of Graubunden. As fat brown cows with elaborately engraved, deeply resonating bells (he said they were worth more than the cows) hanging from their necks mooed through the village on the way to their winter barns, he raised his glass and proposed a toast: "May none of us ever be more than an hour from Gstaad."

Unexpected and unannounced, a savior of bespoke-suited splendor appeared out of the Alpine mists in the person of Richard Sprague, a rich and cunning American entrepreneur, who should have known better. Chairman of National Semiconductor, a big, profitable corporation, Sprague thought the movie business was more romantic than the semiconductor business. He arrived just after Timothy Leary's screen test, when, helped by Sprague's legitimacy and cash, Max von Sydow was signed, along with Pierre Clementi and Dominque Sanda. Many years later, Sprague was to form a company called Wave Systems, which invented a security chip that was supposedly going to be on every computer in the world. According to the *New York Times,* at the height of the Internet bubble, Wave Systems attracted enthusiastic investors who called themselves "Wavoids." Wave became the subject of a formal investigation by the Securities and Exchange Commission, and it was sued by shareholders who accused company executives of making misleading statements to push up the share price. (Sprague's son Steven, who had become the CEO, vigorously denied the accusations.) Before *Steppenwolf* was wrapped up, already disillusioned with show business, Sprague would ask Hamburger: "Who do I have to fuck to get off this picture?"

Finding himself with a real live budget, Hamburger hired Mike to be the *Steppenwolf* press attaché. Mike and Marie-France drove up from the French California to the Beverly Hills of Europe, and set up housekeeping over a kosher butcher in Basel. There they found a production company that had begun as figments of Hamburger's fantasies. Now they were objectified as his minions. He sent flowers to Sanda's hotel room with cards saying, "To my adorable female star." Casting Mike in nonspeaking extra roles. Hamburger told him he was "the first actor to play Tommy Dorsey and Benvenuto Cellini in the same flick."

The book was set in Basel, and most of the movie would be shot there. Although German is spoken in Basel, it is on the French border, and Marie-France did a great take on the Swiss-French accent. She considered it a friendly gesture rather than being impolite. Swiss jokes are de rigueur in France. She was hired to chauffeur the Mercedes sedan Max von Sydow's contract called for. The hotel and most of the locations were in the Centrum and because of an elaborate one-way system discouraging vehicular traffic, driving around central Basel could take longer and be more tiring than walking. Gentleman Max, who loved to walk, permitted himself to be driven because he did not want Marie-France to lose her job. The cultivated actor would leap out and run around to open the driver's door for his cute little French *chauffeuse.*

Hamburger, Haines, and Mike were at a conference table with two executives of Sandoz, the Basel-headquartered pharmaceutical multinational for which Dr. Hoffman worked when he discovered LSD. The room overlooked the Rhine. The business on the table was booking the company's state-of-the-art in-house video recording studio. It was not long after Jean-Christophe Averty had developed blue-box video technology, and Haines's script called for it. As the meeting ended, one of the Sandoz people said: "Mr. Hamburger, I certainly hope we can get together on this, because I'm a big movie fan."

"Well I hope so too," Hamburger replied, "because I'm a big drug fan."

Enter double agent Johnny Staccato. Under his habitual deep cover, Staccato drove on what he fondly hoped was a secret mission back down south to the French California on a short trip to pick up mail and clothes and stuff. Mostly stuff.

He drove back up with a packet of French Connection skag shuffled into the tissues of a family-size Kleenex box placed in plain sight on the floor on the passenger side. Cool—nobody would ever think of looking there.

Understand—these were the very bad, very, very old days. Staccato is long gone. Mike has been an inactive drug fan for years. His nostrils may still twitch at the mention of a toot, and sometimes in bad company in America, he will snort Ritalin, but he doesn't look for it. He figures that if a drug comes to you without asking, it doesn't count as active. Besides, Ritalin is legally prescribed in America—although sniffing it seems to be a gray area. American doctors prescribe Ritalin to preteens for Attention Deficit Disorder. Hand it out like bubble gum. No deficit of attention in America. Stop dreaming and get to work, citizens. Here, take a couple of these. If he lived in America, Staccato might still have a drug problem, but he doesn't.

In France, Ritalin was on the A drug list, the most dangerous and controlled category, along with cocaine and heroin. French and American cultures were pushing in opposite directions. The French medical system encouraged its citizens to lay back and not feel anguished about how hard it is to start up anything. Don't worry about reorganizing the bureaucracy, going to the moon, making better mousetraps. Just calm down. Cocaine, methamphetamine, and uppers of any kind were hard to get in France. Heroin abounded. Methadone could be very easily had with a prescription at your corner pharmacy. The state health insurance even paid for it. French doctors prescribed downers as though they were aspirin. You did not have to ask twice. How many? You want renewable? The French preferred to encourage a kind of collective nod, while America wanted you to stay as wired as possible. Lift that bale, land that contract, tote that barge—don't conk out. Such opposing chemical philosophies explain a lot about communication problems between the two cultures.

Staccato took a secondary Alpine road back up to Basel. It was longer than the Autoroute, but the Belgian hippies said it was an easier *douane*. It was dusk when he arrived at the frontier. A cold wind was blowing down from snow-covered peaks and it had begun to snow in the valley. His was the only car on the French side.

"Hi, *Monsieur l'agent*," Johnny said, handing over his passport: "Nice day, isn't it?"

His New York Chase Bank checkbook came out with his passport, and the agent (he was only a single-agent) asked to see it. He leafed through it and said that, as a legal resident, Staccato was not permitted by French law to have a foreign bank account. François Mittérand's Socialists had recently come into power and smart money was fleeing France. The French franc was threatened. Temporary foreign exchange restrictions were in place. Although he'd have to check with the chief, who was out for the moment, the agent said a *Procés Verbal* would be necessary. (A "verbal process" means a written report; God bless the French language.) Staccato parked and went into the office wondering why an American citizen was not allowed to have an American bank account, but he was too busy trying to look sober to say anything about it.

The agent wound the four-copy form into his typewriter, and asked: "How much cash do you have?" As Staccato took his cash out of his pocket and laid it out on the desk, it occurred to him that sooner or later the agent was going to search him, and maybe his car. Totoche, his friendly, dilapidated gray Opel sedan, was still the only car in the parking lot. It was slowly being covered by the early evening snow.

When the agent's phone rang, Staccato excused himself to go blow his nose. Junkies always return to the scene of the crime.

He was leaning over to make sure the Kleenex box looked, you know, snotty enough, when suddenly the agent opened the passenger door, and there he was leaning in. It was a heroic moment. Bravery under enemy fire, and all of that. Calmly, with a steady hand, Johnny took a tissue out of the family-sized Kleenex box, and blew his nose. Looking the agent in the eye, he took out another and blew again, explaining that he had a bad cold. Then, with great presence of mind, he stuffed a few tissues in his pocket and stood up. M. l'agent blinked and hesitated, but in the end, he only looked cursorily in the glove compartment.

The Procés Verbal was almost filled in when the chief finally arrived. He was big and rosy cheeked—a sort of designer mountain man wearing a trim gray beard, a ponytail, a hand-woven ski sweater, a woolen cap, and wraparound snow shades; his skis were on his shoulder. As he put them down, the agent outlined Staccato's problem. When he'd finished, the chief shrugged: "He's American. He's allowed to have a bank account in America."

It was another example of the trouble you can fall into trying to live in the cracks between systems. The agent asked Staccato if, since it was already completed, he could please sign the verbal statement. It was just for their records. In dire need of a sniffette, Staccato signed without complaint. He never heard from them again.

Back on top of the kosher butcher in Basel, it was dawning on Marie-France that heroin was making her lose her looks. And, in fact, the skin was getting tight over her formerly full cheeks. She enjoyed being stoned even more than Staccato, if that was possible, but she was keeping an even enough keel to recognize that that was exactly the problem. Unconscious, as always, of his wife's true state of mind, Staccato was nodding out over dinner one evening when the thought occurred to him that he and Marie-France were a romantic, adventurous, deeply relevant twentieth-century couple. They had "it" together. "It" being both the "hip" lifestyle—laugh if you must—and heroin. "It" was a profound bond between them. She could never be happy with some square who could not tell the difference between Sonny Rollins and John Coltrane. She would never leave him, because she could never leave "it."

The *Steppenwolf* production moved to Hamburg to shoot interiors. Hamburger loved being in a city called Hamburg. It was a matter of pride that the entire cast and crew should check into the Atlantic, which he called a "fat hotel." By fat, he did not mean overweight, slovenly, out of shape. More like a bulging pay envelope. Smoking a big-budget Davidoff cigar ("it's like smoking money"), Hamburger picked up the phone and ordered schnitzel for fifteen, plus roses for all of his girls, from room service. When an English press junket arrived, and it appeared that there were no vacant rooms, Hamburger tried to bribe the concierge and even the manager, and he paced floors for hours. Finally his face lit up, and he pointed to an imaginary light bulb over his head and said: "Let's order some rooms from room service."

Steppenwolf was destined to become one of the ten best totally unknown major feature films ever made. It was amazing, the extent to which people never heard of this movie. After Sprague took it out of circulation, Hamburger developed a heart condition. It was like a Purple Heart. It went with the territory, and it proved he was a real movie mogul. If you can't stand the condition, get out of the studio. "I have a heart condition," he told everybody. It gave him a good reason to carry all sorts of new medications. He still carried the old ones too.

About a year after *Steppenwolf* had been de-distributed, Hamburger arrived in the French California, loaded with medications old and new. He was out of both focus and sync after an overnight 160-klick-an-hour drive from his habitual jumble of big days and sleepless nights in the big city. Welcoming Hamburger, Staccato told him how happy they were to be living in this peaceful, clean, sparsely populated place. "There are fewer people living here now than there were in the eighteenth century," he said. He drove him around the valley, pointing out the fairy-tale hilltop villages, between which, even in August, when half of Europe descended on the South of France, it was possible to drive without passing another car.

However, whoever named the Vaucluse the French California was misinformed. California implies forward-looking energy, imagination, and money, combined with a sunny, comfortable, laid-back lifestyle. There was precious little energy, not much looking either forward or backward, and the weather wasn't even all that Californian. Laid-back, though, was putting it mildly. You could find a sniffette in just about any hamlet within, say, a twenty-kilometer radius of Les Grands Cléments. The smack was cheap, good quality, and certainly well distributed. It was impossible for Staccato to come in out of the cold. He rode his bicycle to score. The exercise was so healthy, the air so pure. If he felt unhealthy, he could always call for a delivery. Referring to all the hippies selling herb and hard drugs, Hamburger said the French California should be called the "French Afghanistan."

Marie-France's determined survival instinct had kicked in. She suspected that Staccato was one bad habit she did not need. Once she made up her mind, it stayed made up. It got to the point where being "hip" was no longer essential to her. The brotherhood of "it" sucked. The bonds were being unbound. She took pottery lessons, and learned yoga. She became testy—scowling and nagging Staccato when he scratched his nose or his cheek. She'd say: "I don't want to be married to a junkie." He denied being high. He denied everything.

On a rocky hilltop looking down at the lack of action in the French California, Hamburger scratched his head, and said:

"Where do you suppose they all went, M-F?" He called Marie-France M-F. "Where is everybody? Why do you think they all left?"

"How the fuck should I know?" she yelled at him, losing control. She resented him calling her M-F, with its obscene implication. Smart-ass Yankee male chauvinist pig. Fuck Americans anyway. Who did they think they were, colonizing everybody with their so-called culture? And come to think of it, they were living in her country; why weren't they speaking French?

"All we care about is that it's empty," Staccato said, trying to calm things down. "We like it that way."

"I don't like it, Joe," Hamburger muttered, like a black and white World War II warrior: "It's too quiet."

During one of their reunion tours, Mike interviewed Simon and Garfunkel, who were staying at the Grand Hotel, near the Opera. According to the ground rules, he had to talk to them separately—twenty minutes each. Simon was first. One thing Simon said was: "These are the good times. These are the good old days." Mike packed up his cassette recorder and walked four doors down the corridor, where Garfunkel disagreed: "No. These are the bad days. The sixties were the good old days. I wonder what Paul thinks is so dynamic about today. I am very different from Paul."

Simon entered Garfunkel's room carrying a batch of concert tickets. "Look, our pictures are on them," he said. "This is the big time, Artie. Can I use your bathroom?"

Garfunkel said okay, and after Simon went in, he muttered to nobody in particular: "What's wrong with his bathroom?"

11

KENNY G

Mike's journalistic aim was to create his own form. Not a revolution or anything, he just wanted to find his own place where readers could always tell it was him, and he would not have to explain what it was "about."

For example, writing a book about jazz in Europe during the Nazi occupation, he mixed his personal life into the story, trying to make it a good read rather than just another serious history book. What happened to him while writing the book was part of the book. He'd been trying to pull that off for years. Reviewers complained that it was not a serious history book.

In his column, he tried to write profiles of interviewees in the third person that would read as though the subjects had written them. Without quotation marks, you understand. Thus creating a new reality, or at least a new perspective on the old one. It only really worked once, and that was because the subject, Kenny Gorelick, was already a parody of himself. There was not a word in there that Kenny G did not say. Of course, it was a bit of a cheap shot to parody a parody. And in hindsight, the idea is just not practical. To pull it off, you need a combination of a subject somehow worthy of the effort with an unusually successful interview. It was not going to happen often. Arguably, it deserves to be wrapping fish in a barbershop or a whorehouse.

The first time ten-year-old Kenny Gorelick took this neat little sax out of its case and put it together, he thought, wow, this is fun. I'm going to have a great time with this thing.

By the fourth grade he was already the best sax player in his school. The teachers gave him perks and encouraged him. Older guys would ask him how he did this and that and he thought, gee whiz, they're asking me and I'm just a kid. I guess I have a knack for this thing. Teachers patted him on the back and said: "Hey! you're great." And even if he wasn't really as good as all that it made him want to try harder.

Grover Washington Jr. was already making hit records playing the sax. Kenny liked Grover's style. He decided that if Grover could do it, he could make a living playing the sax too. The band director at the University of Washington was contracting musicians for shows that came through Seattle—the Ice Capades, Johnny Mathis, Sammy Davis Jr., Liberace, and so on. The band director took Kenny under his wing. He gave Kenny some calls and it was easy for him. He was the only young musician included with all those older guys. It was fun. It was no problem.

Ten years later, now billed as Kenny G, his albums are getting a lot of airplay on top 40 radio formats and selling over two million units each. *Silhouette* is still on the *Billboard* chart. Grover Washington and David Sanborn are the only two sax players who even come close. Kenny can't really say what's different between his style and theirs, but there must be a difference because he sells more records than they do.

Critics describe his music as bland, shallow, sappy, soporific, and boring. Some people call it "yuppie jazz." Kenny does not believe that "yuppie" is meant in a flattering way. It's not something he'd like to see on his tombstone. But it doesn't really bother him. Yuppies are people who are better educated and get those accounting firm jobs; the advertising executives and the lawyers. He's not saying they are better people, but they need to relax more than blue-collar people. It's fine either way. Nobody's better than anybody or anything but if it's true that yuppies are under more pressure, then his kind of music seems to relax them. It's just a theory he has. Might be 100 percent wrong. Probably is.

It's a question of taste. It so happens at this time that people are inclined to be more attracted to Kenny's music. Kenny imagines from his thirty-three years on this earth that women like softer music. They are the ones who are buying his records. He's sold a lot of records. That's great. But it doesn't mean he's going to change everything because of success and notoriety. It doesn't mean he's going to be a singer or a movie star. People get crazy. They think they can do anything. He's been playing the sax for twenty-three years. He can't all of a sudden do something else.

Sometimes he gets calls to do music that isn't his own. He has to say no. Music is easy for him or he just can't do it. The big hit he had, "Songbird"; it wasn't written to be a hit. That's just the kind of music he writes and it became popular anyway. That's the way it has to be. Easy.

Other guys drive themselves nuts looking for better equipment. He's had the same Selmer sax with the same mouthpiece and the same brand reed since he started. The saxophone is an extension of himself. When he wakes up, he doesn't say let me change my left arm today. If he feels good, his sax feels good. It's part of himself. If neither one of them feels good one day, that's fine, he can live with imperfection. He'd rather go to the movies with his girlfriend than spend time in shops looking for the magic horn. He already has it. He'd rather go swimming, or for a hike or a bike ride. He wants to be a well-rounded person.

He's always thinking about how to become a better band leader. He believes in leading by example. You have to be a good communicator. If somebody has a problem, wait for the right moment and get it settled. It's difficult; the guys in the band are on the road as much as he is. They experience the same hardships. But their rewards are not as great. He's known two of his guys for fifteen years. They're not quite as peerlike as they were. When he comes into the middle of a conversation and they're talking about financing a new synthesizer, they say something to him like, "Go out and buy a Porsche. Come back later." They don't want him around right then. It hurts his feelings but he'll have to live with it. Short of splitting everything seven ways, which isn't fair either. So he tries to give better perks, like flying their girlfriends to Hawaii. But people don't remember those things. Ten days later they're mad at you for not giving them enough per diem. That's just the way it is. He's the boss.

He never listened to Coleman Hawkins and those older guys. Coltrane, that's as far back as he can go. He never learned the old standard songs either. He just started off with the Ice Capades in Seattle and then went right to his own things. If you gave him a page of paper with chords on it, he wouldn't be able to play a note. He watches all those other guys reading those complicated chord symbols and he can't imagine how they do it. He guesses he could learn how if he had to, but he can do his own stuff in his own context better than anybody, and he's getting a lot of radio play. He must be doing something right.

He'd like to live more in the present. He envies people who can stop planning, who don't think about the future, like about what to do for dinner tonight. That's difficult for him. He's always been very motivated. An American Dream guy all the way. Push push push. Try try try. Study study study. One of the guys in the band tells him he should stop and smell the roses.

He'd like to come to Europe to live. He wishes he could learn other languages and other cultures instead of being so isolated and so ignorant. A lot of Americans are ignorant about what goes on in the world. He envies somebody who can speak French. He loves Seattle, though. Seattle's a great town.

If Diana Krall was black, she would definitely have more problems than she has now. And if I was white, it would certainly have been easier. I've been trying to find a way to get past all that.
—Andy Bey

12

MILES DAVIS
A MOUTHFUL OF WORDS

INTERVIEWER: "WHY DON'T YOU PLAY BALLADS
ANYMORE?"
MILES DAVIS: "BECAUSE I LOVE THEM SO MUCH."

Mike was escorted by a trim hostess into the private elevator that goes up to the VIP penthouse floor of the Hotel Concorde Lafayette. When they arrived at the top, she opened the door with an electronic key card, and he wondered if he was locked out or Miles Davis was locked in.

When in Paris, Miles always stayed in the same penthouse, which was of presidential proportions. The Prince of Silence acted like an African king, deserving every inch of his chambers. He was painting now, and it was becoming more than a hobby. Works of art were scattered around the floor and on the furniture. In a hole in the Swiss cheese, Mike was interviewing Miles about painting not music.

"I used to draw Mickey Mouse and that airplane of his," Miles began. "Dick Tracy, he was easy. All I had to do was draw his nose. Flash Gordon, I could do him. I did a drawing of Gerry Mulligan. That was in the forties. Looked exactly like him."

The mention of Mulligan and the forties opened the door for a question which had often crossed Mike's mind about the Birth of the Cool nonet: "Miles, why did you hire me?"

"I liked your sound," he said with his patented croak.

It was an affirmation of the meaning of Mike's existence. Well, not quite. Mike could get carried away. But the fact remained that from "Billie's Bounce," "Israel," *Cookin'*, *Porgy and Bess, Kind of Blue*, and *Jack Johnson* to *Tutu*, Miles Davis had been playing the soundtrack to the movie of Mike's life.

Miles started serious—some say compulsive—sketching about the same time he came off drugs. It was not totally coincidental. Silent, private concentration is often a relief for people who make their living in a collective endeavor that involves public appearance, demands applause, and bothers neighbors. Paint can be put on canvas with a minimum of formal training and provide reasonably fast ego gratification. Painters do not have to worry about collaborators showing up late, stoned, or out of practice. Arnold Schoenberg painted, as did John Lennon, Charlie Parker, Joni Mitchell, Chick Corea, and Tony Bennett. It's harder to imagine going in the opposite direction. A painter in his fifties learning how to play the trumpet would be fighting the odds. Chops take frequent, long, ditch-digging workouts to develop. Learning to play a simple melody is harder on a trumpet than on a piano.

Whatever second art form you are trying to learn, at some point you have to decide on the degree of your investment. Do you have enough desire and energy to do justice to both? Would you be happy to remain a dilettante in one of them? How much insecurity are you willing to suffer? Miles once said that musical training is important mostly in order to learn what rules to break, and so Mike asked him if that was true for painting too.

"The first piano music Art Tatum ever heard," he replied, "were two boogie-woogie piano players playing at the same time on a cylinder. He didn't know there were two of them. He thought that's the way a piano should sound. So he learned how to play like two piano players at the same time. Some guys don't have to know anything about theory because they have something better you can't learn in a book."

He was sketching long, thin women with bright, flowing lines, obviously drawn by somebody with a flair for color and shape, and for women. "The women are moving, doing ballet steps," he said. "I make them with thick thighs and long legs. I like that look. It's the Rio de Janeiro look. I hardly ever draw a man."

When Miles's lawyer walked in with a question, he was greeted with: "You should see a doctor." The lawyer looked confused. Miles, in his sinister bag, explained: "Because you need a personality change." The lawyer left with a raw face. It was not for nothing that Miles Davis was also known as the Prince of Darkness.

He continued sketching flashy, fiery-haired, bright-lipped women with an assortment of felt-tipped pens as he talked. From time to time, he turned his pad around: "You like these chicks? These are Parisian women, you can tell by their sunken cheeks. Speaking French does that. They speak with their tongues out. Language forms your face. What else you want to know?"

His rasp was an emblem of "hip" to generations of hipsters and hippies. It became a badge, like his use of drugs. Eventually, it became "hip to be square," whatever that means, and Miles was out in front once more, a survivor when survivors were all the rage. "Music is like dope," he said. "You use it until you get tired of it. Look . . ."

He sipped herbal tea and continued to sketch sunken cheeks and thick thighs: ". . . I had to stop doing everything." There were no eyes to be seen behind his rose-rimmed shades. His hairline had receded and what remained was suspiciously thick and curly. Miles was the first jazz giant to have a hair transplant. It was difficult to refrain from staring at all that unlikely hair: ". . . Everything."

His voice sounded as though there was a Harmon mute in his throat: "Listen. I was snorting coke, right? Four, five grams a day. Go out drinking brandy and beer around the clock. Get up at midnight. Stay out the rest of the night and half the day. Smoke four packs of cigarettes. Use sleeping pills too. I was pissing blood. I couldn't fuck anymore. I couldn't play anymore. One day I wake up and I can't use my right hand. Can't straighten it out. Cicely panics . . ."

Miles Dewey Davis III, son of a dentist in Alton, Illinois, was married to the Emmy Award winning actress Cicely Tyson. The ceremony had been performed by Andrew Young, the mayor of Atlanta, Georgia, in Bill Cosby's Connecticut home. African-American aristocracy. During their divorce proceedings, Miles accused Cicely of pulling out his hair weave.

". . . Cicely panics. 'Let's go see Dr. Shen,' she says. Acupuncture doctor. Dr. Shen gave me needles. Here, there, here. He gave me herbs to clean my body out. Chinese medicine. I shed my skin; a whole layer of skin fell out. Weird stuff came out of my nose. I didn't know which drug was messing me up so I decided to stop them all. Now I swim forty minutes every day. The only habit I got left is sweets. Cigarettes are the worst habit of all. You're better off snorting coke than smoking cigarettes. I saw Wayne [Shorter] stand there and smoke a cigarette, and I said: 'Why you doing that?' He said: 'I need something to do with my hands.' I said: 'Why don't you put them in your pockets? You got four pockets.'"

What would Miles have done if Dr. Shen had told him to stop playing the trumpet?

"Change doctors," he said, without hesitation.

A French bebop player who hadn't played a new note since 1955 called Mike a traitor when he defended Miles's "rock" period. The Frenchman was a good cat, a fine player, and, an inactive addict, he was fragile. Sadly sipping Perrier alone at a table in a jazz cave in Saint-Germain-des-Pres, he was not a great advertisement for sobriety. He had also worked with Miles in the good old days, and they compared experiences. The French bebopper was one of the many musicians who accused Miles of selling out when he started playing with a backbeat. Mike told him that he had just interviewed Miles, that he thought he was still making the most relevant music of our times, that his rock rhythm section of Al Foster, Daryl Jones, and John Scofield was as good as any he'd ever had, and that *Tutu* was his best recording since *In a Silent Way*. Knowing how much the French cat objected to Miles playing rock, Mike was overdoing it, playing with the bebopper's head. He loved pissing off people he considered assholes; it was losing him a lot of friends, and the cat was pissed off as programmed. "That's your opinion," he said, raising his voice. "It's not an opinion, it's a fact," Mike retorted. The Frenchman rose from his chair, grabbed Mike's lapels, and shook him. He said that rock was the ruin of good music, adding: "You just think you're hot shit because you interviewed Miles Davis." Which, of course, he did.

Not much later, Mike wrote up the interview for a cover story for *Actuel,* a thick, glossy French underground monthly. The magazine was going down-market. Their cover was highlighted by bold pullouts of what the editor considered hot quotes over a photo of Miles wearing his fuck-Whitey look:

I WAS PISSING BLOOD.

I COULDN'T FUCK ANYMORE.

I COULDN'T PLAY THE TRUMPET ANYMORE.

It was yellow journalism, but you don't get to be a big glossy magazine, even underground, by being nice. Famously not nice Miles probably loved it. Mike had always thought that mostly Miles was not nice to people who did not necessarily deserve nice treatment. He would not suffer assholes easily. There was a lot of shit he would not eat. In the end, though, interesting though it may be, Miles's dysfunctional personality is tangential. Frank Sinatra, Stan Getz, and Ray Charles were supposedly not very nice either. And yet they made so much beautiful music. Judge musicians by what they play not say.

Miles's seventies and eighties rock-oriented music has been called "Bartók with a backbeat." He once cited Alban Berg's opera *Wozzeck* as a model for what he was doing: "A window is opened and suddenly the orchestra stops and you hear a marching band from outside. Then the window is closed and the orchestra starts again. That's the kind of thing I want to do. Open some windows. I don't play rock. I don't play jazz. I play *black*. And I'm no accident."

A backbeat is when a drummer accents two and four, the so-called weak beats. This is called binary time, and it is the foundation of rock and roll. The term works better, and is in more current usage, in French—*binaire*. Jazz is based on a more complex and fluid subdivided ternary feeling—*ternaire*. Most Western music said to "swing" has at least an implied backbeat. Playing behind Miles, Philly Joe Jones streamlined ternary drumming by cutting the backbeat in half and only accenting four with a light snare drum rimshot.

When he began to play rock in earnest in the early seventies, Miles forbade his drummers to play ternary time. Not even interludes. And the backbeat was more than implied. It was relentless. Taken together with the merciless wah-wah pedal, it turned a lot of faithful fans off. Although probably not conscious, it was just possible that one reason Miles was attracted to a heavy backbeat relatively late in life was that he had grown bored creating his own grooves. It was a way to continue to be contemporary, and to make money as well (never underestimate Miles Davis's attraction to money). Having others lean on his complex, ternary time for all those years was wearying. He had earned the right to lean on the grooves of others. Let the kids do the work. "Practice onstage," he told them. He followed in the lee of their rock grooves like a bicycle racer in a slipstream.

Picture Miles onstage, his rock band playing a slow blues, his hair weave hanging over his ears, psychedelic green trumpet in hand, slowly shuffling from one side of the stage to the other. The applause is deafening, and he has not played a note. He is being cheered for the blues chorus he is not playing. He puts his mouthpiece to his lips and begins to play again exactly on the first beat of the following chorus. His dance has taken exactly twelve bars. This is a man in time and space at the same time.

In the dressing room, after his tenor saxophonist, Bob Berg, played in a place where he was supposed to lay out, Miles asked why. Berg said that the music had sounded so good, he just had to jump in and play. "But Bob," Miles said: "It sounded good because you *weren't* playing." That's another example of Miles Davis being a not nice guy. Berg was a very good saxophone player, and a sweetheart. Being a minimalist is not always easy.

Mike asked Miles if minimalism was also important to him when he painted.

"I ask this guy who looks after me," he replied: "Michael—he calls me chief. 'Michael,' I said: 'How do you like this painting?' He says, 'I liked it, chief, just before you finished it.' So Mike thinks I spoiled it by painting too much. I have to learn to stop. I know how to stop with music. But there is this problem with balance with paint. It's different."

Miles had begun to paint large abstract swatches of gold, copper, and caked metallic colors with a passing resemblance to Arshile Gorky. Spare, skeletal shapes cavorted on beige, and there were bright circles within colorful squares. When the paintings were unsigned, it was not always clear which end was up. Rock star Miles became famous for the creative color coordination of his stage costumes. "Certain colors fit certain days," he said. "Like I'll want blue all over. But I might change my mind five times before a concert. I always decide at the last minute."

"Does music translate into color for you?"

"You mean do colors flash through my head when I play? You'd be surprised what flashes through my head."

Mike saw Miles for the last time less than a year before he died in 1991. Once more he was in the penthouse suite fit for an African king. He was working on a new incarnation—Miles Davis the actor.

Artwork in progress was again scattered on the floor. Custom-made costumes, designer T-shirts, shopping bags from chic boutiques in four cities, and sound and image reproducing devices were strewn about. The Prince of Darkness and Silence took his castle with him. A gangsta rap video was running on a monitor on a table.

Miles the rock star was having drummer problems: "Drummers are my pet peeve. Maybe I'm hard on them. You always have to tell them what to play, what not to play. If a drummer has fifteen drums, he wants to bang on every one of them. Some drummers drop the tempo so they can squeeze in all of their favorite fills. I might have my son play drums with me." (It was said that his son was reluctant.)

Miles the painter had designed a logo for Hennessey cognac ("they're sponsoring a lot of jazz this year"), and he was working on a large black, white, pink, and brown collage that included rusty nails, pieces of driftwood, and bamboo. "You can hang it on your wall if you have a big house in the Hamptons," he said: "Are you following me?"

He was in Paris to star in the movie *Dingo*, directed by Rolf de Heer, a Dutchman, with a Franco-Australian production crew. It was to go the way of *Steppenwolf* the movie, and *A Case for the Balkanization of Practically Everyone*, the book. Unavailable, out of the catalogue, remaindered, on the floor of that cosmic cutting room in the sky.

Dingo takes place in Paris and Australia. It begins when a big jet carrying Billy Cross (Miles) and his band to a gig in Perth is temporarily grounded on an isolated airstrip in the outback. The entire population, about seventy, of a nearby mining camp comes out to see the four-engine flying machine. To kill time during repairs, Cross's group sets up on the tarmac and plays for the people. A ten-year-old named John Anderson in the crowd is mesmerized. As the musicians get back on the plane, he runs up and says how much he liked it. Cross, who lives in Paris, tells the boy to look him up if he ever gets there.

The boy grows up to be a trapper of wild dogs, called dingoes, that prey on sheep. He practices the trumpet in the outback. Weekends, he leads a friendly country and western band named Dingo and the Dusters. He has a recurring dream in which Billy Cross keeps saying, "Come look me up in Paris." But he's stuck; he has obligations. After some coincidental events change his life, John Anderson flies off to Paris.

Miles objected to the clichéd roles offered to black actors. Pimps, for example. Which had not stopped him from playing a pimp on *Miami Vice*. Miles had his price, and basically he admired pimps. Pimps were cool. Sean Connery, who is nothing if not cool, admired the coolness of Miles. Here he was basically playing himself. "So twenty years pass and this kid comes to see Billy Cross in Paris," Miles said. "He is married by now, with two kids of his own, but he wants to find out if he's good enough to be a professional trumpet player. 'Don't ask me,' I say. 'You got to find out that stuff yourself.' So I take him down to this club and tell the guy there to let him sit in."

Cross has had a stroke, and he no longer plays jazz on the trumpet. Programming synthesizers by the time Dingo tracks him down in Paris, Cross has become a smooth-jazz star. Dingo's enthusiasm inspires Cross to want to improvise again. Michel Legrand wrote the soundtrack, and on it Miles the movie star plays over loose, ternary, walking 4/4 time—something Miles the rock star had sworn he'd never do again. Miles makes *Dingo* not as bad as it looks.

Miles had aged. He was shrinking. Dexter Gordon had nicknamed him "Wisp" after a journalist described his trumpet style as "wispy." Now, after kicking all those drugs, Miles was beginning to look Oriental—as though he was overdosing on Chinese medicine. His skin was getting yellow. You could see scars from his miscellaneous accidents, assaults, and operations through his loose-fitting, translucent, super-lightweight white shirt. He moved infrequently and with difficulty. His face was younger than his body, thanks to cosmetic surgery, and to his hair weave, which appeared to be growing a pompadour. Periodic burps ("Pardon me") were age-old tics more than bad manners.

"Michael!" he called to his aide-de-camp Michael Elam: "Am I sixty-four or sixty-five?"

"You're sixty-four, Miles."

No longer able to drive a car, he had begun to feel "shaky" living in his four-million-dollar oceanfront house in Malibu, so he'd bought an apartment on Central Park South.

"How's living in New York again?" Mike asked him: "Is there still all that greed?"

"Where? In Brooklyn?"

"On Central Park South."

"What greed? It's always been like that. I don't know really. I don't go out that much."

The following evening, the *Dingo* crew was dining in a temporary tent raised on the sidewalk near their shoot next to metro Saint Paul in the Marais. The mixture of Australians and Frenchmen reflected the nature of the coproduction. Director Rolf de Heer went to great lengths to make it clear that this was not repeat not a jazz movie. No aficionado, he seemed wary of the minority nature of jazz. "It's not a genre film. It's deeper than that. Each one of us at some time in our lives wished we would have done something else, or we have had a dream we never executed. We say, 'I wonder what would have happened if I'd done that instead of this.' Dingo is lucky, he gets a chance to try and follow his instinct before it's too late."

Yaphet Kotto had been de Heer's first choice to play Billy Cross, but there were scheduling problems. He had been on the verge of signing Sammy Davis Jr. before the entertainer grew terminally ill. Miles and Sammy (no relation) Davis were friends, and Miles had flown out from New York to Beverly Hills to say goodbye to Sammy on his deathbed.

In his book *Miles and Me*, Quincy Troupe quoted Miles describing "how morose everyone was in Sammy's house, how it felt like a death watch, and how it made him feel so sad. Then, when he went in to see Sammy, he thought on how thin Sammy was, and how big his head looked atop that tiny body. Miles said he could think of nothing else to say, so he just spoke the truth; told him what he was thinking right then and there, saying, 'Goddamn, your head looks so big, Sammy, sitting on top of that tiny little body. Man you betta eat something, 'cause you look real weird right now.' He told me that everyone in the house was appalled at what he had just said, but that Sammy had instantly broken into hysterical laughter when he heard Miles's words; that Sammy laughed so hard, for so long, tears running down his face, that Miles got worried . . . Sammy called him the next day to thank him for being so truthful and for bringing some much needed laughter into his final days."

Until a friend suggested it, it had not occurred to de Heer to cast Davis the trumpeter as Billy Cross. He was only vaguely familiar with Miles's music. All he knew was that his reputation for reliability was not good. But a number of people he respected were "keen on Miles. So I met him and decided to take the risk because I saw that if we could pull it off, he'd burn the place up. He's a natural actor. Every day he gets better. He learns more, he's faster. He's intelligent and instinctive at the same time. He's on time, co-operative, and he knows his lines. He's easy to work with. Nobody around here has ever seen that 'other' Miles, the nasty guy with the bad reputation. His sense of timing is phenomenal. You start to feed him his next line because he seems to have forgotten it, but then he comes out with it at just the right time. And he leaves you with a mouthful of words you don't need."

"Cop Killer" was taken as a threat. I was surprised. I had not really been aware that so many people all over the world hate cops. It became like an anthem. I was introduced to this aboriginal chief in Australia. He was really old, in his nineties. When I walked in, he said immediately: "Ice T— 'Cop Killer.' " This is a guy who might say three words a year. How did he know about "Cop Killer"? And you know what else he said? He said: "The police are not the enemy. The law is the enemy." In other words, don't hate the player, hate the game. I didn't choose the game. The game chose me.
—Ice-T

13

FREDDY HEINEKEN

HE BREW

I'M SORRY, I HAVE TO SPEAK IN ENGLISH. SEE, I'M
AMERICAN. WE DON'T LEARN FOREIGN LANGUAGES. BUT
THAT'S WHY WE'RE SMILING ALL THE TIME. YOU CAN SEE
US COMING DOWN THE STREET, YOU KNOW. HEY! HI!
HOW'S IT GOING? WE'VE GOT THAT BIG SHIT-EATING
GRIN ON OUR FACE ALL THE TIME BECAUSE OUR BRAINS
AREN'T LOADED DOWN.

—MICHAEL MOORE, MUNICH, GERMANY

For Freddy ("'y' not 'ie,' and why not?") Heineken, bad jokes were
an art form   more of an affirmation of life than a series of stories.

He said he played "good tennis and badminton." He liked sexy
songs like "I'm in the Nude for Love." He liked Mendelssohn, he
also like Mendel's father. Freddy felt a "special rapport" with Jewish people. He wanted—"this is my best bad joke"—"He Brew"
written on his tombstone.

"Brewery Magnate Dies at 78" was the title of his obituary in the
International Herald Tribune in January 2002. After which a black-
framed announcement from the family arrived in the mail: "With
feelings of great sorrow and loss we regret to announce the death

of our beloved husband, father, father-in-law, and grandfather Dr. Alfred Henry Heineken."

Freddy died the richest person in the Netherlands. He had maneuvered his family's eponymous beer into a prominent place in the mass market and had a personal fortune of $5.6 billion. Heineken shares were known as "Freddies."

He had also been a songwriter, record producer, and jazz fan, and when Mike met him in a recording studio in Blaricum, an upscale Amsterdam exurb, Freddy was sixty-seven. Freddy had already spent "countless desperate sessions" in the Blaricum studio —which is on Bierweg (Beer Street)—auditioning Euro-crooners who sang "de" instead of "the" and "luf" for "love." The object was to record an album of Freddy's ballads, to be called *Dreamscape*. Freddy had a hunch that there was a "big hole in the market for pretty ballads." Freddy would have liked "my friend Frank Sinatra" to sing them, but that was not going to happen. He would have liked to have written more songs, but he had been busy building his father's brewery into such a successful giant that "some people think I can walk on water. This is not true. I walk on beer."

Freddy had been kidnapped for three weeks in 1983. It was a front-page story. Gangsters not terrorists, the kidnappers demanded a ransom of more than ten million dollars. "I stayed sane by telling jokes to those jokers," he said. "They never laughed. They thought I was out of my mind. They expected me to be whining not winning." He said, only half joking, that the kidnappers settled for less ransom because they could not stand to hear any more of his jokes.

His jokes were dear to him. He put his word games and twisted sounds "into little drawers and they hop out at just the right moment. What's the difference if you've heard them before? They're so stupid. I roar with laughter and congratulate myself—'that's funny, Freddy'—even when there's nobody around. Words are only sounds. Playing with sounds is a musical sort of game. Music is a language."

Music as language is an old jazz tradition. Jon Hendricks and King Pleasure made up lyrics to instrumental improvisations like Wardell Gray's "Twisted" and James Moody's "I'm in the Mood for Love." Jazz argot became a major influence on spoken English, from "Jim" to "man" to "dude." The adjectives for "jazz" went from "hot" to "steamin'" to "cool." Paul Desmond, who was very cool, who played the saxophone with Dave Brubeck, and who was a friend of Freddy's, had a good ear for verbal licks. Freddy and Paul used to sit around and tell each other stories. Paul told Freddy the one about his high-fashion model girlfriend leaving him for a financial analyst. "Sometimes models go around with musicians for awhile," he said. "But they usually end up marrying a banker or a broker or someone with real bread. This is the way the world ends, not with a whim but a banker."

The man who walked on beer could really appreciate stuff like that. He loved the company of musicians. Freddy said that one nice thing about producing and writing songs for *Dreamscape*, and about his musical activities in general, was that for once he wasn't the boss's son. Mike had been in a similar situation. The difference between them was that Freddy was a fox: he could concentrate on two things at the same time, while Mike was a hedgehog, and could not.

There were times when Mike wished he could afford first-class air travel, thousand-dollar-a-night hotel suites, and two-thousand-dollar hookers. When he was president of his father's steel company, he had driven a Mustang convertible and lived in a duplex he co-owned in a fancy townhouse in the West Village. But the psychic price was too high for the physical luxury involved. He decided to sell his share of the house and get out of the steel business.

On his way down-market, Mike sublet Paul Bley's rent-controlled loft on Hudson Street, and he would remain flagrantly low maintenance for the rest of his life. The lack of ambition was appalling. He flew tourist class, traveled around town on public transportation. His Parisian office was in an unpaneled, cobwebbed, poorly ventilated cave. He thought of it as a womb. The bamboo plants on his terrace were allowed to wither and die. Let it be ratty. Content with so little, and having had so much more, Off-Season Charlie was fascinated by the richest man in the Netherlands.

Freddy Heineken had invested $125,000 of his own money to finance his pretty-ballad hunch. He finally found a good cruise-ship crooner named Kenny Colman, who was billing himself as "the last saloon singer." The album was orchestrated à la Nelson Riddle and released by the Dutch record company Dino. There are no Freddy jokes on the album. Freddy stopped joking when it came to music.

The completed album required a song plugger, which was a role for which he himself would have been perfectly suited. During the two years he'd spent in the U.S. as a young adult, Freddy had been seduced by American advertising and marketing techniques. Compared to the staid world of Dutch business, it had been liberating. Freddy could sell beer in Bordeaux. Actually, what Freddy plugged best was optimism. It was hard to keep a straight face in his company, and Mike soon stopped trying. Lighting one unfiltered Gitane cigarette with another, Freddy said: "A doctor advises an ailing man to stop drinking and smoking. The man asks, 'Will I live longer?' The doctor says: 'No, but it will seem longer.'"

Freddy's father was a "top-notch classical pianist." Growing up, there was both a Bechstein and a Pleyel in the Heineken salon. Beethoven was played on the Bechstein, Chopin on the Pleyel. It was lunch with Yehudi Menuhin, tea with Toscanini, supper with Bruno Walter. The only trouble was that "with that kind of music

I always knew what was coming next. I like to be disturbed, surprised. And that's what jazz is all about."

Jazz was considered "vulgar" around the Heineken house, so he readily admitted that his love for it possibly included an element of generational revolt. As a young man, he had followed Coleman Hawkins around when the tenorman lived in Amsterdam ("Boy, was I a groupie"). Herbie Hancock "often came to visit." Listening to the Belgian harmonica wizard Toots Thielemans, who solos on *Dreamscape*, affected Freddy's tear ducts. "I don't listen to Toots's music," he said. "I absorb it." Freddy took Stan Getz to lunch: "When Stan played, it was like he was not even there; the music came from a little man inside him somewhere." He knew Gene Krupa and Buddy Rich. He liked drummers: "I fool around with drums and I have a good sense of syncopation. I once played the conga drums with some black guys in Jamaica. You know, the pink tourist in the ugly shirt? I can do that. They asked me back. They bought me drinks."

While Heineken was semiretired by the time Mike interviewed him, he did not feel as though he was at the end of anything. He was always trying to learn something new. "Who wants to be the world's biggest expert on clothes hangers? If that is the limit of your ambitions, you are in trouble."

Richard Vague was CEO of First USA Bank, with thirty-two million customers. It would later be bought by Banc One for eight billion dollars. Vague's ambition was to have his employees function like Miles Davis's band. Everything comes back to Miles Davis. Miles knew very well that money was a sign of reality. But only on his own terms. Taking money for playing a pimp was just hustling the Man. He knew that the more outrageous his monetary demands, the more respect he would get from the white music business, and the more they would spend to protect their investment. He knew his own worth.

Now it seemed that Miles and money went together in an institutional sense as well. Was this a major alienational shift? Had whims become bankers? "Miles Davis dominated jazz music in the late fifties and sixties," Vague explained to his side people during a corporate motivational conference. "The jazz scene then was characterized by groups of three to six pieces, typically including drums, bass, piano, saxophone, and trumpet. They would play either an original song or a popular composition such as "My Funny Valentine," and they would reinvent that song with extended improvisational solos, new chords and harmonies, syncopation, tempo changes, and complex interplay. The boldest, most daring thing about Miles—the thing that set him apart from almost all his contemporaries—was that he always, always hired musicians who were better than he was. Better technically, better composers, better improvisers."

Vague explained that the musicians were all so accomplished and got to know each other so well that anybody in the group could take the lead to slow down or step up the tempo, and the others would follow. Innovation could come from anyone, anytime, anywhere. He did not want his people explaining that they do certain things "just because Dick Vague says so."

"Now," he concluded, "I'm not nearly so naive or presumptuous to think that there is much of an analogy between Miles Davis's group and First USA. But we must have the very best people, and we must have the kind of supportive, inclusive environment where the very best can thrive. We aspire to many of the things characterized by Miles's band."

The establishment's relationship to jazz made history during World War II, when jazz-loving Germans used to say: "Anyone who loves jazz cannot be a Nazi." Basically true, this was also somewhat self-serving. Just as not all black people are lovable, and not all football players are dumb, not all German jazz fans were anti-fascists. A Luftwaffe ace was known to have tuned in his radio to the BBC jazz program before bombing the antenna. Still, the music became a metaphor for freedom. It was mistrusted and even feared by both Hitler and Stalin. That jazz was considered subversive by the power structures running two of the ugliest and most repressive regimes of the twentieth century is a big compliment to the music. Attending jazz concerts in occupied France was an antiregime statement that was just about risk-free. There were Wehrmacht uniforms in Django Reinhardt's audiences. Nazi officers loved Django, and they were happy to believe it when they were told that he was playing French folk music, not jazz. They had more important things to worry about. German jazz musicians changed the name of "St. Louis Blues" to "Sauerkraut," called it German folklore, and went on playing the same song the same way. Although there were all sorts of rules forbidding syncopation, jitterbugging, zoot suits, and so on, by definition, it was almost impossible to censor improvisation. In spite of being persecuted, or because of it, jazz had a mass audience in Nazi-occupied Europe and behind the Iron Curtain. It never had more respect before or after. The enemy of my enemy is my friend.

"It wasn't easy [in Nazi Germany] being a Jew playing Negro music, even if your name was Adolph," Eddie Rosner once said. Born Adolph, and also known as Adi, and as the "white Louis Armstrong," Eddie Rosner was a hot trumpet player and leader of a popular swing band with good arrangements and soloists, first in his native Berlin and then, after the Nazis chased him out in the late thirties, in Warsaw. After building two successful, top-flight swing bands, he was forced to move still further east when the Germans occupied Poland—to Soviet-occupied Bialystock. His third band was dubbed the State Orchestra of the Byelorussian Republic by First Secretary Panteleimon Ponomarenko, a jazz fan who named Rosner an "honored artist" of the republic. The morning after the Rosner band gave a mysterious command performance in what appeared to be an empty theater, their manager received a message that Stalin had been in the balcony and had enjoyed himself. The story got around, and they toured the Gulag and military bases during World War II known as "Stalin's Band."

After the war, Rosner's music came to be defined as bourgeois capitalist propaganda, and he was sent to the Gulag. When he was released, he tried to form another band back in West Berlin, but he had lost the desire, and the touch, and he died pretty much forgotten.

Like Eddie Rosner, Freddy Heineken did not reject an idea simply because it had never been done before. And like Richard Vague, he did not believe in eliminating the element of risk. The Heineken sales department thought Freddy was out of his mind when he proposed selling beer to the Third World in square bottles. He called it the "world bottle." The emptied bottles could be used as bricks to build cheap houses in hot climates. It was like starting a jazz band in Byelorussia. Freddy's board turned him down.

According to his obituary in the *Economist:* Freddy "was born Alfred but the name Freddy stuck from childhood. The name seemed to suit his engaging personality, his love of life and his rough sense of humor. A woman journalist he was showing around his Amsterdam headquarters—it is called the 'Pentagon'—was mildly surprised by a picture in the bedroom next to his office of a naked woman with a cat, entitled 'The Woman with Two Pussies.'"

Freddy was "serious about not taking myself seriously." He was "bored by the beer business. I like business. I work supremely fast. I like to work. I can read a thick tax file in a half hour and retain everything in it. I didn't have that much choice about it. My father and grandfather were in the brewery business; they'd built it up. Why throw it away? And I liked the job. Basically it comes down to the quality of people you gather around you. All businesses are basically the same. The music business is not that different from the brewery business. There's manufacturing, distribution, advertising. Anyone can learn business logic. When I say that, it doesn't make me very popular with other businessmen. They expect to be well paid on the assumption that what they do is difficult. But there's nothing very mysterious about business."

Insecurity was not one of Freddy's problems. Security, however, was. After his kidnapping, he had to begin driving around with bodyguards in a bulletproof Rolls-Royce. Mixing his ballad album in the Blaricum studio, he lit his last Gitane, crumpled the pack, and threw it against the wall. Immediately—seamlessly, without a word—one of the jar-headed Dutch hulks protecting him came and picked it up, and handed him a freshly opened package of Gitanes.

Freddy pointed to him and said: "I put quarters in these guys."

He lit up. "I wonder if Einstein smoked," he said. "You know, it's not smoking, it's worrying about it that gets you. The only thing I worry about is boredom. That's where music comes in.

"Do you know the story about the musician's baby? Right after it's born, they put it on its back. There's a violin on the left side, and a pile of gold coins on the right. If the baby reaches for the violin, it's going to be a musician. If it reaches for the coins, the baby is going to be either a banker or a thief. If it grabs both, then it's going to be a songwriter."

Not one of the obituaries mentioned anything about Freddy Heineken having been a songwriter.

"You can't lie," my teacher Jaki Byard once told me. What he meant was that you can't fool the people. If you sit there and just run between these different bags you took from a bunch of other players, you are in fact trying to hide your true self. Maybe you're afraid you don't have a true self to express. In that case, what you're playing is really saying is, "I'm a musician with an identity crisis." On the other hand, when you're direct and honest and lucid, they're going to know that too. You can't lie and you can't hide. It can get very intimidating.
—Brad Mehldau

14

SERIOUS MUSIC

KULTURE IN THE GOYISH ALPS

THERE'S A VERY NARROW NOTION OF STRENGTH IN THIS
COUNTRY. IT'S ALL CONNECTED TO MILITARISM; KILL
ANIMALS, CHOP WOOD WITH AN AX.
—DAVID PALETZ, POLITICAL SCIENTIST AT DUKE
UNIVERSITY, QUOTED IN *USA TODAY*

"Extraordinary cultural hideaway; castle and hotel in spectacular
Alpine valley one hour south of Munich," is how Schloss Elmau ad-
vertises itself in the *New Yorker:* "Concerts with internationally ac-
claimed artists, dances, great sports, skiing and health spa, indoor
and outdoor pools, saunas, lakes and rivers."

Mike's magnificently comped room had high ceilings, wood
paneling, antique furnishings, and a view of a Bavarian Alpine
mountain he came to consider his own. Grateful, he tried not to
bleed on the carpets. His feet were rotten; it could get bloody. The
operator of a bed and breakfast in Manhattan had been so furious
about her bloody carpet that she never even asked Mike what was
bleeding. As far as she knew, it could have been his heart. There
were mountain walks you wouldn't believe. During a heavy early
April Bavarian snowstorm, Schloss Elmau's guests were stuck inside for three days. When the weather cleared, the white slopes of

Mike's mountain were blinding to look at in the afternoon, and the peak was bright orange at sunset.

Dietmar Muller-Elmau, the owner and manager of this Grossinger's-With-Kulture in the Goyish Alps, was a German intellectual who liked jazz and Jews. Thank God for German guilt. Having made his fortune with Fidelio, a computer software program for hotels, he sold it and returned to the Bavarian village of Elmau, where he'd grown up, and took over the management of Schloss Elmau from his father (his grandfather had built the place in the early twentieth century). Some guests were saying that his father had had something to do with the S.S. They were not sure of the details, but it kept coming up. Dietmar maintained it was more complicated than that—his disillusioned father had left the National Socialist party before the start of World War II. Sensitive, aware, responsible Germans such as Dietmar were proof that for once the Americans did something right. Billions were spent to make the Germans peaceful people. And it worked. A wide reader and an explosive laugher, resembling a solemn Jeff Bridges, Muller-Elmau sponsored series of political debates and concerts. He invited Israeli, Arab, American, Scandinavian, and German scholars and historians to his hotel for conferences on such subjects as "Challenging Ethno-National Citizenship: Multiculturalism and Immigration Regimes in Germany and Israel." Regular chamber music concerts were scheduled, from Mahler to Mehldau. Not all of Muller-Elmau's relatives and partners approved of Jews and jazz being featured in the family hotel. The heirs were feuding, a court battle was threatening.

By far the majority of the fearlessly bourgeois guests seemed to be entirely satisfied. Seating was random in the dining room. Mike kept breaking sausage with strangers. They were alarmingly polite and positive. The fresh, delicious, plentiful, and vehemently un-kosher food was displayed temptingly on buffet tables. Able to take as much as they wanted, people ate too much. They talked about eating too much. Many had been here before, many of them many times. One married couple was celebrating meeting in this very building thirty years earlier. They approved of Schloss Elmau's family atmosphere and courteous service, the clean air, the mountains. Mike and one coincidental table-mate—a middle-aged lady wearing pearls—discussed the ECM recording of the Hilliard Ensemble singing the madrigals of Gesualdo. A well-tended, cultivated, elderly woman, whose place card read "Frau Zimmer," asked Mike how he'd liked the Robert Schumann recital the previous evening. "Schumann is a bit too German for my taste," he replied. That wasn't even true. Why did he say that to the poor woman? Some part of him—the French part, no doubt—did not want Germans to feel too good.

Schloss Elmau guests were an attractive balance between the elderly, the just-right, and the small (few teenagers). Three generations played board games in the sitting rooms. The children remained at the dinner table until excused, but then they ran around and played and made noise like healthy kids anywhere. They were well-behaved, bright, attractive, blond, blue-eyed children who were a pleasure to have being children around you. Still, it was all too easy to imagine the children in this place, say, seventy years earlier—just think what can happen to well-behaved, attractive, blond, blue-eyed children.

Martin Lovett had driven down with his wife from their home in Hampstead, London, in their Bentley. Retired after having been the cellist with the prestigious Amadeus String Quartet—named after and specializing in the music of Wolfgang Amadeus Mozart —for more than twenty years, he was an Englishman of Russian-Jewish descent whose ancestors, like Mike's, came from a shtetl near Kiev. They agreed that if they went back far enough, chances are they would find they were related. Chatting through the buffet and coffee, Mike and Lovett were served by young men and women, mostly from the Balkans, who came to Germany on short work permits to learn German and the hotel trade by doing work the Germans no longer wanted to do. The boys were pimply and awkward and testosterone-driven. The girls were rosy-cheeked and ripe. With their Teutonic *mädchen* uniforms, they looked like farm girls.

A string quartet of three handsome young German women wearing revealing gowns and a male cellist in a tuxedo performed Schubert's *Der Tod und das Mädchen* (Death and the Maiden) one evening. Why were the girls' shoulders and arms bare while the cellist was totally covered? The temperature in the room was the same for all of them. How can they object to being regarded as objects when they plead for objectification? Watching the bare arms and shoulders of the maiden bowists performing *Death and the Maiden* was not disagreeable.

Martin Lovett did not attend. The next day, he seemed proud of it. He was tired of music, or perhaps he was trying to convince himself to be. He did not want to hear about other cellists. Although they were the same age, both having just turned seventy-five, and they knew each other, Lovett scowled at the mention of Miroslav Rostropovich, who was still active. Trying to demonstrate that he was reasonable, Lovett said that he liked Yo-Yo Ma. When he'd met him, Lovett had asked Yo which one was his first name. "I don't know," Ma replied.

Mike identified with Lovett. He had stopped playing in public when it started giving him more pain than pleasure. Lovett had retired when he'd had enough of the professional musician's life. Mike and Lovett were both retired English-speaking professional septuagenarian musicians. That should have been a bond. Music is, or ought to be, a brotherhood. Both Mike and Lovett had been awarded a Chevalier in the French Order of Arts and Letters. They were both knights, royalty—family. In fact, equal or not, they were certainly separate. They had lived closely parallel lives without ever touching. Except for Schloss Elmau, they would probably never have met—one example of what makes the place special.

Talking to Lovett was a rude wake-up call to the fact that classical musicians still apply the literal, superior definition of the term "serious music." In Mike's world, the term was unambiguously ironic; it was understood to be between quotation marks. Nobody took the concept of "serious" music seriously in the world of jazz. While Lovett never questioned it. He was *serious.* The way Serious musicians think, everybody likes Duke Ellington and the Beatles, and Brahms may have been right when he said that there are only two kinds of music, good and bad, but jazz musicians deal with a simple short form, one they make up as they go along—and they play out of tune. Where's the discipline? When jazz musicians tune up and it's almost there but not quite perfect, they say, with irony: "Good enough for jazz." If being out of tune means you are going to sound like Fletcher Henderson or Charlie Parker, that's close enough. While the Unserious dismiss the Serious: "They sure do play in tune." Meaning they sure don't swing.

Swing, says the Irish musicologist, teacher, and bass guitarist Ronan Guilfoyle, is "how musicians relate to a groove." He defines a groove as "the generation of good musical feeling through rhythmic means alone." We are talking about music, not social attitudes. A "swinger" has a hard time relating to a good groove. "There is no such thing as a bad groove," says Guilfoyle. "The music either grooves or it doesn't. A groove is its own reward. It does not necessarily have to go anywhere. There are many sorts of grooves— Count Basie's four to the bar, George Clinton with Bootsy Collins on bass, Tito Puente's Afro-Cuban music, the Modern Jazz Quartet. Groove and swing are African concepts, and they are largely alien to European classical music."

Guilfoyle was born and bred in Dublin, and his jazz treatments of traditional Irish folk music were once considered so revolutionary that a friend called him the "Irish Salman Rushdie." He teaches musicians and music lovers how to become what he calls "rhythmic beings," starting with the fact that "African music is based on the interlocking of polyrhythms."

With the increasing popularity of so-called world music, unusual time signatures have become more common. Musicians have had to learn how to be comfortable in as many of them as possible. Guilfoyle's area of expertise has been growing more mainstream. He lectures on "rhythmic counterpoint" at workshops, and he teaches classical instrumentalists, including members of the London Symphony Orchestra, how to swing. He insists it's possible. "For the jazz composer, the first rehearsal involving classical musicians can be a frightening experience," he has written.

What seemed easy and effective on the page is ruined by a lack of any kind of cohesive rhythmic feel by the players. Cues are missed. Half the players are early, half are late, some rush some drag. How can this be? These are highly trained musicians. In jazz, we use the term "time" as if it is a given that everyone understands what that means. We say this guy has "great time" or "I don't like that guy's time feel." But if asked to explain what we mean, as I once was by a classical musician, it's actually quite hard to do. I think what we mean is this—when we talk about someone's time, we are referring to the way the player's notes relate to the underlying pulse of the music. If the player has a very strong relation to the pulse, we can feel the power of this person's "time"—it will be strong. In that situation we can feel ourselves being moved emotionally simply by the way the notes

are placed in relation to the pulse. There can be many different ways of relating to the pulse—in front, on top, behind, with
a particular attack. All of these different feels are possible, and
players who relate to the pulse in many different ways can be
said to have "really good time." So it's not the specific relationship to the pulse that is the common denominator for good time.
What is it then? It's the ability to place one's notes in a consis-
tent relationship to the pulse. I've often noted that with classical
musicians, their relationship to the pulse can vary wildly, even
within one measure. It is due to a lack of rhythmic training.

The concept of swing being African, it was alien to Martin Lovett. He was a thoroughly European musician. While swing was
at the center of Mike's life. Serious musicians were interpreters
—translators, you might say. Their insurance was paid up, they
planned for retirement, they discussed trading futures during rehearsal breaks. Although interpreting existing music may be more
serious, it is also less creative than making up your own.

The difference between the two of them became evident when
they exchanged their autobiographies. Lovett gave Mike a copy of
a glossy public scrapbook he'd self-produced about his professional
life with the Amadeus String Quartet. Mike gave him a copy of
his remaindered memoir, *Close Enough for Jazz*. Looking through
Lovett's photos of, texts about, and testimonials from his friends
and colleagues and celebrities in the classical music world, Mike
could not find one personage who was in both books. They were
cast in two entirely different movies. Their exchange of Benny
Goodman stories added up to serious schizophrenia—and a metaphor for their untouching parallel lives. Lovett's stories involved
classical music situations, Goodman rehearsing for performances
of Bartök, and so on. Lovett painted the clarinetist as a sweet, com-
passionate, respectful colleague who loved to play classical music,

respected classical musicians, and had once paid for an Austrian violist he did not know to be flown home to Vienna for surgery when he became sick in Philadelphia.

Meanwhile, a jazzman who'd played with Goodman had told Mike: "To those who didn't know Benny, anything you say against him is like insulting Christ. To those of us who did know him, it's like insulting Mussolini." Benny called his band members, some of them in their fifties, "my boys." He called his singer Helen Forrest "my girl singer." She called him "the rudest man I ever met." Goodman once told Johnny Guarnieri that he was the worst pianist he had ever heard, reducing him to tears. "Benny treated everybody like slaves," bassist Bill Crow said. "Regardless of race, creed, or national origin." After Goodman's prestigious tour of the Soviet Union for the U.S. State Department, Zoot Sims was asked how it had gone. "When you're with Benny Goodman," Zoot said, "every tour is in Russia."

"Zoot who?" Lovett asked.

When the Lovetts checked out of Schloss Elmau, the roads were still icy from the early April snowstorm. He hired a local taxi driver to help him get his Bentley up the frozen hill and on the road to Garmisch, the nearest town of any size. He said it was impossible to find snow tires for a Bentley. With his newly installed cutting-edge GPS system, Lovett did not have to worry about taking the wrong autobahn. Mozart had been very good to Martin Lovett.

The Swedish Esbjorn Svensson Trio (EST) arrived later the same day. Just passing through, they were not performing during this visit. They had a deal with Dietmar where they agreed to a cut rate for their concerts at Schloss Elmau in return for just-passing-though privileges. Another thing that makes the place so special. During their previous night's concert in Munich, a listener had remarked that they were "simply the best jazz group in the world." The *Economist* magazine had just said something similar about them. A recent article in the French weekly *Telerama* had claimed that the best jazz in the world these days was coming from Scandinavia.

It cannot be repeated too often. There is no best. This is not football. And if there were a best, to be bitchy about it, it would probably not be EST. When Mike asked them to name their favorite trio, they answered in unison: "The Police." Which surprised him. It was superbly politically incorrect. Mike liked them for it. Touring German rock clubs, they had been listening to the Police in their van. The Police were a good rock band, and, although you might have expected EST to prefer Keith Jarrett, they had been thinking a lot about the youth market. Whatever their reasons to choose to play for young people, good pianos were not part of the rock club tradition. Svensson tried to keep his sense of humor about sticky, uneven, untuned actions. It took a lot of imagination and effort— with Edgar Varèse in mind, he could sometimes use the badness of pianos as a source of inspiration. After struggling with a disreputable instrument in an otherwise respectable five-hundred-seat theater, the classically trained Svensson encountered the arrogance of "serious" music. "If I had known you were such a serious pianist," said the theater director, "I would have given you our number one Bechstein concert grand."

Mike's last evening in the Goyish Alps was spent listening to a recital built around the theme "Mozart in Minor." Mozart rarely wrote in minor keys. The program included a piano composition in memory of his mother, who died while the two of them were in Paris for the premier of his *Pariser* symphony, which was not well received. In a letter to an Austrian friend that was read aloud during the recital, Mozart wrote that, despite all the bad things that had happened: "I still love Paris, and I wish I'd never have to leave."

What used to be called "comparative musicology" is called "world music" now. The ivory tower is connected to the street. This is to a great degree due to Alan Lomax, who went to the Delta, the prairies, the prisons, the bayous—out of the way places where something substantial was going on in American folk music. I am so proud to have worked with him. He recorded bluesmen, railroad workers, chain gangs, cowboys. At the time, that was not even considered music. It was considered anthropology. How wonderful it was to find music where there wasn't supposed to be any music.
—*Roswell Rudd*

15

MELVIN VAN PEEBLES
GONE FISHING

I THINK I'M BETTER OFF NOT SOCIALIZING. I MAKE A
BETTER IMPRESSION IF I'M NOT AROUND.
—CHRISTOPHER WALKEN

If you took three zeroes off Melvin Van Peebles's income, divided his fame factor by about five, and ignored skin color, he and Mike were not unalike. About the same age, they had both been involved with words and music, and with the world known as "hip," and both of them had fathered sons with French mothers.

Mike met Melvin during rehearsals for the musical review *Melvin Van Peebles et Ses Potes* (and His Pals), which he had cast, and was directing, choreographing, singing, and starring in. "I shoot the breeze between numbers," he explained. "Sort of like Charles Aznavour." Van Peebles did not suffer from stage fright.

The review featured him singing his own songs and gospel and rhythm and blues adaptations of the songs of the neglected nineteenth-century cabaret artist Aristide Bruant. This one performance in the *Café de la Danse* would be the end of it. Van Peebles harbored secret hopes for a subsequent Broadway run, but the odds were against it, and, anyway, he did not need the money. "I don't have a mistress and I don't have a car," he said. "As Thoreau said, you're rich in relation to what your needs are."

Mike's mortgage had been paid off. He felt like a millionaire spending up to a hundred dollars, like part of the middle class up to a thousand dollars, and over that he was definitely poor. He was retired every day until noon. Although he could buy a Saab, it would break him. The concept of low overhead is more upscale in the wide world of talking pictures, in which Van Peebles is best known. What was considered Robert Altman's down-and-out period in Paris in the nineties included a chauffeur-driven sedan, entertaining in expensive restaurants, and a stylish Left Bank apartment around the corner from François Mittérrand.

Perhaps he did not have a mistress or a car, but Van Peebles maintained residences in New York, Los Angeles, and Paris. He had risen to the level of what was called an "iconic presence" after he produced, directed, starred in, and wrote the music for *Sweet Sweetback's Baadasssss Song,* a movie about a black man on the run after killing two white policemen. It was dedicated to "all the brothers and sisters who have had enough of The Man." Bill Cosby loaned him fifty thousand dollars, and eventually the movie grossed more than fourteen million. Nevertheless, Van Peebles was not particularly proud to be credited with spawning Hollywood's "blaxploitation" trend. "The term really has nothing to do with me," he said. "It has a derogatory sense to it. Everybody tries to keep us in our place with these limiting labels."

While a student at Ohio Wesleyan University in Delaware, Ohio, the future "godfather of black film" was, he recalled, "once sent to Coventry." He had had an attitude problem: "The right people on the campus boycotted me. But, you know, I felt sorry for them being denied my company." Obviously, the problem was their attitude not his. Now he was writing another novel—his thirteenth book—on speculation. "If the manuscript is rejected," he said, "the way I look at it, it will be the publisher being stupid."

Mike felt any rejection to be well deserved. Rejection was to be expected rather than a surprise. He would credit his unsure grasp of reality. Perhaps his writing had not been clear, or commercial, enough. Or a sloppy manuscript—formatting counts. The possibility of the problem being that the publisher was stupid would not occur to him. His fear of rejection became self-perpetuating, attracting more rejection. Whereas Van Peebles's confidence was so strong that if a girl he was courting turned him down, he would be sure that "she's an obvious lesbian."

Having the crown of his head shaved one rainy morning on Rue de la Roquette, Mike heard Bob Marley's "No Woman No Cry" on the coiffeur's radio. He'd never understood the lyrics before, not that he'd tried very hard. Treating pop lyrics as deep metaphysical truths was really dumb. However, the idea of "no woman no rejection" made sense to him. One of the positive things—maybe the only thing—about being over seventy was that it was possible to admire female architecture without a cool-destroying, rejection-risking erection. Old age was a voyeur's paradise. Were young women aware that they were all beautiful? Was Mike aware of that when he was young? Were they all beautiful when he was young? One way or another, it felt good to be free of them. Remembering women he had had may in fact have been better than having them.

Van Peebles's macho self-certainty was in part a number—some sort of "bad brother" shtick. The self-confidence was real enough, though the macho was at least partly faux. He dared you to look behind the social roles it amused him to play. The characters were tempered by the sweetness of the "bad" intonation of his speech, and by the ironic twinkle behind black-rimmed Harold Lloyd eyeglasses under the pulled-down visor of a 1930s James Cagney gangster cap. With his grandfatherly gray beard, laid back hipster manner, and wide frame of reference, Van Peebles reminded Mike of Melvin's fellow icon the late Slim Gaillard. Melvin placed a respectful hand over his heart at the mention of Slim's name.

You may have been skeptical when you heard Slim Gaillard say, "I invented the word groovy," but few would have disputed his claim to be the father of the Voutie language, which went something like this: "Voutie oroony macvoosy ohfoosimo." And there is no doubt that he wrote hit songs called "Flat Foot Floogie (With a Floy Floy)" and "Cement Mixer (Putti Putti)." You might have raised your eyebrows when he told you, "There are two pages about me in Jack Kerouac's *On the Road*," but there they are: "One night we went to see Slim Gaillard in a Frisco nightclub. Slim Gaillard is a tall, thin Negro with big sad eyes who's always saying 'Right-orooni,' or 'How about a little bourbon-orooni?' In Frisco, great eager crowds of young semi-intellectuals sat at his feet and listened to him on the piano, guitar and bongo drums . . . Now Dean approached him, he approached his God; he thought Slim was God."

When Gaillard was a guest on the Bob Hope radio show, Hope asked his other guest, Marlene Dietrich: "What do you think of Slim Gaillard?" "Vout," she replied. That's a fact; he had it on tape. But now you are forced to take his word: "Ronald Reagan used to come in with Jane Wyman when I was working at Billy Berg's in Hollywood; even Ronald Reagan was saying 'vout.'"

He worked in the speakeasies: "Way before bebop; way, way, far far far before—many many many far before bebop. Al Capone loved musicians. Maybe some of his other activities were undesirable, but he was always very nice to me." There is hard evidence that Gaillard once led a band called Henry Sausage and his Pork Chops ("We fry, man"), and that the sheet music to "Flat Foot

Floogie" went down in the 1939 New York World's Fair time capsule, along with "The Stars and Stripes Forever."

When a theatrical agent told him, "You're just the type I need for a part," Gaillard objected, but not too hard: "I'm a musician not an actor." He ended up with roles in the television series *Marcus Welby, MD; Mission Impossible; Medical Center; Charlie's Angels;* and *Roots* ("I played good guys"). His daughter married Marvin Gaye — Gaillard claps his hands in the background on Gaye's album *Sexual Healing.* Gaye was afraid of flying; he was thinking of canceling a big tour because of it. "I consider you like my dad," he said to Gaillard. "What do you think I should do?" Fortunately, Gaillard was also a hypnotist.

Van Peebles had been a street musician and a journalist in Paris, a portrait painter in Mexico, he studied astronomy in Holland. Gaillard had music publishing companies in London and Los Angeles, he owned fruit orchards near Tacoma and real estate in Miami. Van Peebles was the first African-American trader on the New York Stock Exchange. His book *Bold Money: A New Way to Play the Options Market* was still in print fifteen years later. Van Peebles and Gaillard both had successful careers as businessmen and actors. And they were both veterans of the U.S. Air Force. Gaillard studied hydraulic and electrical systems while with the Tuskeegee Airmen, the World War II African-American fighter plane squadron. He used to "practice taking engines apart and putting them back together again day after day using minimum tools and minimum light." Van Peebles was the navigator and only black crew member on a B-47 bomber in Korea. "The other guys all had thick southern accents," he recalled. "But you would have thought I was an albino, the way they treated me. They were unbelievably nice. They'd say, 'Y'all got to come down to our barbecue on Saturday.' Because they knew that if the navigator makes a mistake, everybody dies." Melvin was reminded of his B-47 crew when both Halle Berry and Denzel Washington won Academy Awards. "Basically they owe their Oscars to Osama Bin Laden," he said. "When Americans are in trouble, suddenly we're all Americans."

Van Peebles could read, write, and speak French; he translated his own books. His telephone answering machine message, in its entirety, went: *"Ouah. À la pêche"* (roughly, "Yeah. Gone fishing"). His French had an African-American accent, which was chic in France. He had been called a one-man conglomerate, an enfant terrible, and a Renaissance man. Van Peebles had just finished acting one of a continuing assortment of character roles—in this case, "a gangster in a movie that doesn't have a name yet."

"I have various arrows in my quiver," he said. He has been called a precursor of rap. Released when that sort of thing was still filed under "spoken word," his album *Ain't Supposed to Die a Natural Death* influenced the Last Poets and Gil Scott-Heron. Van Peebles's soundtrack music for *Sweetback* was performed by Earth, Wind & Fire, and it became their first album. Jon Pareles reviewed his cabaret act *Br'er Soul and Roadkill* at Manhattan's Fez café in the *New York Times:* "Van Peebles turned rock, pop, Broadway and disco songs into extensions of his own down-home philosophy. As he sees it, most of us are roadkill on the highway of love."

"Roadkill on the highway of love" is just another way to say no woman no cry. Having an almost sort-of ex-wife for a best friend is one way to be with a woman without ever crying about it. Mike managed to cry anyway. He and his buddy Marie-France went to see the Robert Guédiguian movie *Marie-Jo's Two Loves.* Set in Marseille, the film's Mediterranean images are beautiful. Good-looking good actors play deep and mature characters. Marie-Jo, the heroine, cannot make up her mind between her loving husband, who runs a small construction company, and her lover, a virile harbor pilot named, of course, Marco. She is deeply in love with both of them. Marie-Jo, an attractive, sensual woman of a certain age, mother of a teenage daughter, wears minimal makeup and has had no apparent surgical lifts. Mike really did hate to say anything nice about the French, but he looked at Marie-Jo and thought how well French women age. Marie-Jo and her two lovers say important things to each other in beds and kitchens. She decides to leave her husband and teenage daughter and move in with Marco in his romantic studio overlooking the harbor. Although he had begun to suspect something, her husband, a good, honest, loving man, is totally shot down. Her daughter throws a fit, and screams that she'll never speak to Marie-Jo again. During some dreamy weeks in a lover's paradise overlooking the port, the Frogue bitch (sorry) seems to be content at last. But when Marco goes out of town on a short business trip, she lasts all of two days before returning home to her husband.

In a corner café after the movie, Mike teased Marie-France: "That's a French woman for you. Go out of town for two days and she leaves you." M-F was not in a teasing mood. The way she saw it, the picture was about this deeply romantic and interesting mature woman, and it treated a universal subject sensitively. Obviously, Mike would never understand French women.

To him, it was some sort of Monty Python French-lover skit: "How do you get your *femme* to leave you?"

"Go out of town for two days."

The English are good at making fun of the French. Mike had clipped an article in the *Guardian* that said the French think truffles and Camembert smell like sex. The article said you could probably wave a slice of toast at the French and they'd think it smelled like sex. He read it to her. She did not laugh, which was disappointing, though not unexpected. Marie-France was Mike's only good friend in the city in which he was stuck. The degree of her importance in his life was hard to exaggerate. Every day involved a conscious effort not to call her. It was embarrassing to keep telephoning your only friend in town. She had a boyfriend, who probably also kept telephoning her. Lately, Mike had been wondering if it might be a good idea to pull away from Marie-France, to become less dependent on her. The idea might be looked at, if you looked at it cross-eyed, as a healthy exercise in letting go. A way to lighten the load, get rid of earthly burdens, and so on. We die alone, and if Mike was already alone, there would be less to lose. Some sick shit.

He had been letting friends go one after the other, a string of them, over a period of years. The dying alone justification came after the fact, it was not premeditated. Maybe it was his friends' fault, though he doubted it. It had been an extended social decrescendo leading up to that inevitable big fermata in the sky. His revolutionary pal Sal was tough, smart, and intense, and he had one wild eye and his cheeks were always stubbled. His father had been a colonel in the Republican army during the Spanish Civil War. Sal had taken tea at the Coupole with Jean-Paul Sartre and Simone de Beauvoir. He knew Huey Newton and Carlos Fuentes. When not teaching university students how to tear down the system, Sal speculated with Left Bank real estate. He borrowed the money from fellow revolutionaries like de Beauvoir. The excitement of waiting until the last minute to pay them back gave him a rush (he did not do drugs). Sal asked Mike to lend him twenty large. Mike was living off interest, and Sal considered interest reactionary. One definition of a counterrevolutionary is someone who won't lend money to a revolutionary. Then there was Artie, who ran an ad agency in Paris. Artie invited Mike for weekends at his big country house in Champagne, in the woods an hour northeast of Paris. Both of them loved jazz and they could talk about it for hours. Then, one night, Artie wanted to put on a record by a country singer he said was different from the others. Mike said please don't. Artie put it on anyway. Mike liked Willie Nelson as well as anybody, but he was feeling pushed. His sickly sensitive shit-detector went off, and he heard himself tell Artie to go fuck himself. It went back and forth like that for a while, and neither one of them ever made an effort to make up.

Mike's long leakage of friends was also due to his having moved around so widely and often. Or his friends had moved. Or he or they started or stopped taking one drug or another. Marie-France suspected that it had something to do with a competitive vibe Mike threw out without realizing it, and then got caught up in. After being at a festival in Switzerland for four days, he returned, and there was not one message on his answering machine. It may have been a bit extreme, but it was not really surprising. Mike could be awkward, passive, grumpy on the telephone. Melvin Van Peebles probably got messages like *des petits pains*. Normal people keep their friends, and go on making them. Melvin certainly returned phone calls, and probably went out of his way to be friendly and cooperative. Most folks must be like that. In part, it depends on the definition of a friend. People tend to promote acquaintances. Having a large number of friends is important to them—it's a sort of social greed, quantity over quality, immediate satisfaction; similar to a CEO's obsession with a fat quarterly bottom line at all costs. One thing was sure: Melvin Van Peebles was friendlier than Mike.

The idea for the Van Peebles and His Pals musical review was born when he was invited to a film festival in Nantes. He thanked them for thinking of him, but said he didn't have a film that year. "No, you don't understand," the festival's director replied: "We want you to be the entertainment." Having nothing better to do at the moment, and being "too short to play basketball and too nervous to steal," he took out the sing-dance-plenty-hot arrow from his quiver and cast six young Nantais singers and dancers to be his *potes*. Leaving them some demos before a fast business trip to Los Angeles, he told them to "get as close as possible to the arrangements." When he came back, he was more than impressed: "Oh, man, man, man, man, man! These people are terrific. They are so talented and positive. They really want to do it the right way. Like Quincy Jones says: 'You've got to leave room for God in these things.' For once God got it right."

Mike thought that maybe, God willing, he'd made a new friend. He and Melvin thought along the same lines, had comparable heroes, and they seemed to like each other. It was agreed that it would be nice to get together again. When Mike picked up the receiver and punched out Melvin's number, the answering machine said that he'd gone fishing. Mike left a message suggesting dinner, but Melvin never returned the call.

Barbershops & Whorehouses   XV

I've had it. I've been here too long. You have to follow the music. This expat thing is over.
—*Steve Lacy, before moving to Boston after thirty years in Paris.*

16

WAYNE SHORTER
BEYOND A SMILE ON A FACE

THE MOMENT OF FINDING A FELLOW CREATURE IS OFTEN
AS FULL OF MINGLED DOUBT AND EXULTATION
AS THE MOMENT OF FINDING AN IDEA.
—GEORGE ELIOT, *DANIEL DERONDA*

"I'm not interested in a man," Marie-France told Mike before leaving him: "I'm interested in *men*." She probably didn't mean it the way it sounded—she was only trying to say that she was being faithful in her way. Parisian women regard sex as a sort of workout routine, a martial art, yoga—good for the digestion and the complexion. At least that was their reputation. He thought of her words often because they were a defining example of what he did not understand about women of any nationality.

"You're not as hip as you used to be," she said. "Married people should be three—me and you, plus the two of us together. We're not even one anymore." He had told her that in the first place. Leaving him, she threw it back in his face. It was a pretty good line. And so Marie-France became the third woman with whom he would not have minded growing old to leave him. Why did they all leave? When she said she'd "found somebody," it sounded like the happy ending at the end of the rainbow. Was Mike supposed to congratulate her?

She asked him to move out. Obediently, he started to look for a studio to sublet. Talk about a jerk. When Mike told his shrink, Dr. Pomme—he was being analyzed in French—about the separation, the good doctor looked surprised. He asked Mike how come he had to move out since M-F was the one who had "found somebody." Dr. Apple saved his life; thanks to Dr. Apple, he was no longer vulnerable to women. The idea of a late-in-life romance was laughable. "I must laugh at myself," Nathaniel West wrote in *The Dream Life of Balso Snell:* "And if the laugh is 'bitter,' I must laugh at the laugh. The ritual of feeling demands burlesque and, whether the burlesque is successful or not, a laugh."

While he was a fan of not taking yourself too seriously, Mike failed to see any burlesque in his situation. He felt abandoned, unloved, unlucky, *insortable.* The chemical tug of war between Mike and Johnny Staccato was getting brutal. It was costing him too much money, his health, and his marriage. So his mind was not exactly on his work when he went to the Ritz hotel to interview Herbie Hancock and Wayne Shorter.

It was good to see good jazz musicians catered to in the power bar of the Ritz. Herbie took the role of, so to speak, the speaker of the house; Wayne was the power behind the throne. Both practicing Buddhists, they had played with Miles together. They were close friends. They were performing in duo, and their improvisations were abstract, contrapuntal, and very subjective. When Herbie said he preferred to play the same tunes in the same order every night because it "eliminates one of the variables," Wayne added helpfully: "There are more constants."

"We can concentrate on . . ." Herbie began.

"Concentrate on Constance," Wayne finished for him, grinning.

"There's more to Wayne than meets the eye," Herbie said. "Wayne writes with simplicity, but there's always that spice of his in the voicings he chooses. And he writes them . . ." He paused for emphasis: "with a pen. Not a pencil—a pen. I learned back in 1967 when we were doing *Neffertiti* with Miles . . ." He turned to Wayne: "Remember? I learned I'd better pay attention to playing Wayne's exact notes. There's always something in there you have to learn."

"I shift the weight of the notes sometimes," Wayne explained softly. "The way the ninth chords move, for example. I call it my 'nightclub sound.'" His voice resembled the refined texture of his saxophone tone, but the decibel level was rising as the Ritz bar filled up, and he was getting hard to hear.

"Was that nightclub or ninth-club?" Mike asked.

"Ninth-club?" Herbie laughed. "That sounds like something Wayne *would* say. That was a Waynism."

After coffee, Herbie had to leave for another appointment. It remained for Mike to interview Wayne. Instead of asking him about future plans, recent triumphs, and the state of the music, he heard himself sigh and start to talk about how depressed, rejected, and strung out he was. High on self-pity, Mike laid out his tale of woe. Wayne was quiet, thoughtful, generous, a good listener; his eyes fixed over Mike's shoulder. He knew about emotional pain. One of his children was autistic, and his wife had been killed when TWA flight 800 crashed on the way from New York to Paris. And Wayne was an open and welcoming person, so Mike kept talking. He related to Wayne as family, both of them being sons of Miles and all.

When Mike had finished, Wayne asked him: "Why do you like certain women?" Not waiting for an answer, he continued: "Think about it. You're always building your own report card. You can get an 'A' in love. An 'A' in recognizing the one woman who you should promise to be with. That's good fortune—recognizing her. You're fortunate. A lot of people don't even recognize the woman they should promise to be with. Now that you've had a couple of rehearsals, you can remember your past, and help get your future straight. You can be in charge of your own report card."

In his introduction to *Footprints*, Michelle Mercer's biography of Wayne, Herbie Hancock wrote:

> In his jovial way, and with an innately uncanny sense, Wayne says what a person needs to hear in order to expand himself. No, it's even better than that. It's more like, you feel that Wayne has gleaned deeper meaning from a question by using it as a spring-board for an answer that will "knock your socks off." And per-haps change your life for the better. As a matter of fact you might start to think, *Wow. I didn't know my question had so much to it.*
>
> Wayne is a transformer. He exudes such honesty, purity, trust, and respect for others that he can transform, elevate, and awaken your life while you're both having fun. Wayne trans-forms people all right, and he gets better and better at it. It's as though he's aware that it's safe to be honest, pure, and trusting. It's a source of light. He sees that inside everyone, and wants to let that light reveal itself in others. He takes you outside the box and into expanded possibilities.

There was no interrupting Wayne, and he was picking up speed: "You can build new karma to erase negative karma from the past and make your own destiny. It's cause and effect, based on deeds and actions. A lot of people have the wrong idea about karma. Karma does not mean destiny. 'I did a number of things today so that I built a certain amount of karma for the future.' It can come from way back—from karma you built over a long period of time.

"I went through a period when the other aspects of my life were depressed and there was only music. I started to become very aus-tere. I stopped smoking. I don't smoke anymore. Only when I'm drinking a glass of wine. Maybe I should stop the wine too. Herbie and myself . . . some other people—Tina Turner—started to try and figure out what people 'accomplish' in their life. What are the states that dominate a person's life? Musicians usually try to stay in a state of rapture. Musicians love rhapsodies. This is part of your problem.

"People envy musicians because it seems like they're always having a good time. But a roller coaster takes you where it goes; you don't take the roller coaster to go where you want to go. You get to that high point and people start to scream. It seems like you're all having a good time. But I found out that a state of rapture can turn very fast into a state of hell. All of a sudden you're screaming for real.

"At first, there was only music for me. But other aspects of my life like family relationships kept coming to the surface, and then music took the passenger seat. It became very difficult to sit and write a piece of music, and I didn't know why. I'd been out on the road for pretty much thirty straight years, and I was in no hurry to go back. I read books, watched ball games, sat in the sun, learned about computers, and read up about the future. Do you know that in the future we will have medical smart rooms with robotic facilities and fail-safe systems in our homes? We won't even need to call a doctor any more. Vehicles will be automatically directed on smart highways. And we may not even need smart highways anymore after the invention of enough stuff like medical smart rooms. The only way to go out of your house will be by the eject button. Bam! May Day! Straight up.

"So I'd be staying with the same eight bars all day, and it turned out to be a blessing. My whole life was being transformed into something more powerful. More complex. I could no longer rely on the same short fantasies—you know, those nice little wispy songs I used to write. Not that I'm writing earth-shattering music or anything, but I might have stayed in those comfortable green pastures forever if the personal pressure hadn't forced me to relate to the entire world, and learn how to really drive my own car. I get letters from people. I got a letter from a woman who said my music made her want to be a better mother to her child. Another one said, your playing makes me want to go out and grow better carrots.

"See, there are ten states of enlightenment. Total enlightenment is the eternal indestructible nature. Indestructible happiness. Beyond a smile on a face. What I'm saying is that you are probably in one of the six lower states—anger or self-absorption, for example. Throughout history, most people have been captive in one of the six lower states. People dominated by learning and intelligence are usually the hardest to get into a state of enlightenment, because they think they know it all."

It was a mouthful. Transcribing it, Mike was appalled at the condition his condition was in. What self-indulgence. Why had Wayne taken the trouble to answer him in such depth? They hardly knew each other. It was astonishing to hear Wayne's words played back. There may have been good karma, but there was no article. (He wrote an article anyway.) It was his own fault, with all of that sons of Miles nonsense. Why did everything always come back to Miles Davis? If the transcript was accurate, and there was no reason to doubt it, not programmed to hear such enlightening words, let alone respond to them, or act on their implications, Mike had been starving, but, at the same time, he had been too out-to-lunch to open the door for room service. Then it was too late to do anything other than a sniffette.

Barbershops & Whorehouses XVI

Insecurity is the fountain of youth.
—*Gil Evans*

17

ORSON WELLES
PATCHED AND PEELED IN MOGADOR

THE PROBLEM IS IT HAPPENS OVER TIME. LET'S START
WITH JANUARY 1ST. LETS DO DOPE FOR THE FIRST TIME.
YOU WON'T DO IT AGAIN FOR MAYBE A MONTH.
FEBRUARY YOU'LL DO IT TWICE. MARCH 3 DAYS IN A
ROW—AND ONCE MORE AT THE END OF THE MONTH.
APRIL, MAYBE NOT AT ALL. MAY, 5 DAYS IN A ROW THEN
SKIP THREE. THEN 10 DAYS IN A ROW AND SKIP 3 AGAIN.
YOU CAN CHOOSE WHAT DAYS YOU DO IT SO
NATURALLY THERE MUST NOT BE A PROBLEM. WITH
EVERYONE SOMETIME AT LEAST ONCE A YEAR SOME SORT
OF CRISIS HAPPENS—THE LOSS OF A FRIEND, A MATE, A
RELATIVE. THIS IS WHEN THE DRUG TELLS YOU TO SAY
FUCK IT. EVERY DRUG ADDICT HAS SAID FUCK IT MORE
TIMES THAN THEY CAN COUNT.

—KURT COBAIN'S DIARY

In the sixties, when a New York publisher commissioned Mike to
write a book about recovering addicts, drugs were still part of a
jazz critic's area of expertise. He was good at research. Following
a larger than life bouncing ball going faster than the tune, he was
beginning to do interesting things, like cocaine and heroin. They
made him insecure, but insecurity is the fountain of youth.

One thing he liked about Orson Welles was how he created money out of nothing and lost it without thinking twice. "Welles admitted that he was an anachronism," Peter Conrad wrote in his book Orson Welles: The Stories of His Life: "He likened himself to a corner grocery store that had somehow endured into 'this age of supermarkets.' In fact he was closer to the subsistence farmer who supplies the grocer, laboring with the aid of an extended family whose members are rewarded with goods (champagne dinners, five-star hotel rooms, limos, cigars) rather than salaries. Needing to find an alternative to the studios, with their tedious emphasis on cost-efficiency, reliability and the mass-production of look-alike artifacts, Welles restored the economy that preceded industrialism; a feudal system in which there was no need for money because business dealings were regulated by barter."

A barter economy. Perfect. What could be more marginal? In sixties New York, when Dr. Feelgood (a doctor you went to when you may not have been feeling exactly bad, but you wanted to feel *good*) agreed, for a fee, to allow patients to add a speck of cocaine to his more or less legal mix of vitamins and speed, Mike stepped right up. *Esquire* magazine had just published his profile of Walter Winchell. Returning to his Union Square loft from the good doctor's uptown office, it occurred to him that an *Esquire* feature about Orson Welles would be a cool career step. Well-fueled for the Big Apple, he worked the phone fast and fearlessly until he tracked down the heroic subsistence farmer in the Beverly Hills Hotel. Welles picked up the receiver, and Mike said who he was, and what he wanted, and was he interested?

"Not at all," Welles replied, and quickly hung up.

A sobering experience. Mike did not like sobering experiences. There would be as few of them as possible in the decades to follow.

His alter ego Johnny Staccato—you remember the under-deep-double-cover secret agent doing all those sniffettes in Pigalle—

originally took over the wheel of the ship when Mike began to steer clear of the company of others to keep them from trashing his high. Staccato was going to say fuck it more times than Mike could count.

Please forgive the dirty words and the multiple identities. They are clumsy devices, and probably cop-outs, but there's a lot to cop out from. Staccato had become one weary Warrior of the Substances by the time—the mid-eighties—he flew from Paris Orly, via Casablanca, to Essaouira on the Atlantic coast of Morocco. Orson Welles's daughter, Beatrice Welles-Smith, was throwing a big bash to celebrate the release of a newly remastered print of her late father's film of Shakespeare's *Othello*. Invited guests included Dennis Hopper, Ruth Warwick, and the international press. The film had been shot in Essaouira, then called Mogador, and it had won the Palm d'Or at Cannes in 1949 before going out of circulation. The new print was to be premiered on Essaouira's town square.

Because of a series of personal and personnel disasters, Welles had moved production from Rome to Venice to Mogador, where the ancient ramparts were a cheap place to film Shakespearean exteriors. Shooting would be interrupted as he dashed abroad to play roles in *The Black Rose, Prince of Foxes,* and *The Third Man* in order to make the money to pay everybody. It would become a way of life. The Irish actor Michael MacLiammoir, who played Iago, and who wrote a book called *Put Money on Thy Purse* about waiting for Orson in Mogador, described the director, who considered a motion picture a "ribbon of dreams," as having "a glare like a dangerous dark-brown bull." Because there was no money for costumes, Roderigo's murder took place in a bathhouse with actors wearing sheets—it was hailed as a stroke of genius.

"Mogador's Jews carried Welles on credit," said a toothless old fellow named Nimero, an extra in the movie who now spent his time sipping tea in the shade on the main square of the town now called Essaouira: "They were the tailors and the carpenters; the craftsmen who made this town alive. We didn't want them to leave. Other Jews told them to leave. Since the Jews left, this town is zero. Kaput. Mogador lost its soul."

And Staccato was in the process of losing his in Essaouira. He had convinced himself that his soul was safe from any Faustian deals so long as he stuck to those cute little harmless sniffettes. Junkies who fix consider sniffers sissies—cowards, not to be taken seriously. Staccato took vitamins, made sure to drink a lot of Evian water for his liver and his spleen, and he never in his life mainlined (except in Dr. Feelgood's office, but that was legal so it didn't count). That sniffettes were nonaddictive was a given, not to be questioned. It turned out to be an alarm system on the blink. Some souls take forever to answer their wake-up calls. Mike was over fifty before waking up to the fact that when women admired his decorative small hands, as they often did, they might be speaking in code about a smallness elsewhere. "Yes, my hands are small," he'd say, agreeably: "I can hardly span an octave on the piano." Had he woken up sooner, he could have said: "But I have big feet."

He had awakened to the flaw in the sniff-myth in Toulouse, only a few months before his trip to Essaouira. He was researching an article for the KLM in-flight magazine about the airline's Airbuses. On the flight down from Orly to Toulouse, where they were assembled, he realized that he had forgotten to score. *Merde alors.* This was no minor oversight. Oh well, maybe forgetting about the powder proved he was not terminally under deep double-cover. He could come in from the cold whenever he wanted. One smack-less day was no big deal. He dismissed the passing thought that there had not been many of them recently. He was good at dismissing passing thoughts. Anyway, he'd be at his dealer Ricky Cheval's place in Pigalle that very evening. In the long run, he thought, forgetting to bring along a supply was probably a sign of good health. Although, it would soon be clear, not in the short run.

Under his straight-journalist cover, double agent Staccato was met at the Toulouse airport by an Airbus press officer who gave him brochures, cost comparisons, specs, and so on. Shown around the giant assembly hangars, he asked probing questions, and took copious notes. Toulouse was booming with Airbus-related business, and the press attaché took him to lunch in a humming expense-account restaurant packed with suits cutting deals.

When Staccato sneezed into his sautéed rabbit, he thought: "My goodness. I must be getting a cold." His nose was running, his head began to pound. Then the chocolate mousse rose back up his throat. He was feeling kind of seasick. Was the food bad? Did he have a fever? Had he remembered to take his vitamins?

Aha! Cheval's code word for junk was "vitamins." Staccato realized exactly what it actually was that he had not remembered to take. So here it was at last, the dreaded thing. Someday you have to come down. Recognizing the cause of, and remedy for, his malady, he was so relieved to have diagnosed it that he overlooked its terminal implications. He was good at overlooking terminal implications. The best he could hope for in the immediate future in this provincial city was a bottle of Neo-Codion cough syrup. You could get Neoc in any French pharmacy—with disapproving looks, but without a prescription. It tasted rotten, you had to drink two full bottles to get your edge off, and it was constipating. The Airbus press officer drove Staccato around Toulouse in search of cough syrup. It was Monday, and French shopkeepers close on Monday. When a pharmacy they finally found open was closed for lunch until four-thirty, Staccato's straight-journalist impression became no longer viable. He asked to be taken to the airport immediately so he could catch an earlier flight to Paris. With dopey luck, the airport pharmacy was open; Staccato had a peaceful nap, and caught his originally scheduled flight back to Orly.

You'd better believe that a couple of months later, on his way down to Essaouira out of the same airport, this time for a whole week, Staccato was not taking any chances. Carrying his stash through Moroccan customs, he recalled his adventure with the Kleenex box at the Alpine frontier. How lucky he'd been. Now he was flooded with fear. Not fear of getting caught—fear for his life. Fifteen years later, and here he was still smuggling heroin wrapped in Kleenex. What a dumb trip. Where had his life gone? There's a story about a young executive who gets a promotion, and moves his family from the Upper West Side of Manhattan to Beverly Hills. The family is deliriously happy about the weather, the palm trees, and their spacious house. Before driving his new Mustang convertible to his first day in his new office, the executive takes a dive into his new swimming pool. When he comes up, he's sixty. Staccato preferred to ignore such complicated questions as what he would be doing when he was sixty. He was good at ignoring complicated questions.

During a small lunchtime script conference (the conference was small, not the script, though that too) on the Faubourg St. Antoine, Staccato's nose had nodded into the soup as he was charting plot points. The African-American actress with whom he was conferring, we'll call her Alma, jumped up and said so the whole restaurant could hear that she was not going to collaborate with some smack-addled hipster. Alma, who knew a nod when she saw one, fired his ass then and there.

It was a treatment for a movie about Valaida Snow, a flamboyant sister who sang and played trumpet and led her own band touring between Shanghai, Cairo, Amsterdam, and Chicago in the thirties. Alma wanted to play Snow, who rode in her orchid-colored Mercedes wearing an orchid suit with a pet monkey wearing an orchid cap and a chauffeur dressed in an orchid uniform. Snow remained in Europe too long. She was arrested as an enemy alien by the Nazis, and spent two years in a camp in Denmark before being released as part of a prisoner exchange. It was a great story. Alma was perfect for the role.

Finding himself no longer associated with Alma, Staccato lost no time moving into denial. He had great moves into denial. "To move is not difficult," Alexander Trocchi wrote in *Caine's Book:* "The problem is; from what posture? This question of posture, or original attitude; to get at its structure one must temporarily get outside of it. Drugs provide an alternative attitude." Staccato loved alternative attitudes. He rationalized: "She's on a star trip . . . It's not enough money . . . it's getting to be too much like work . . . I'm too busy with other jobs . . . It'll never get out of preproduction anyway."

Alma was, of course, right to cut him loose. Staccato was around the bend, off his rocker, the lights were off, there was nobody bloody home. Following the advice of Stephen Daedalus, he was practicing "silence, exile, cunning" for survival, Staccato was taking silence and exile to new heights. Forget about the cunning. Forget about survival. His "fuck it," nose-in-the-soup number was reaching the point of no return. Heroin had become an unfortunate necessity, something like condoms.

When people in Essaouira asked Staccato why he was wearing shades at night, he replied, with attitude: "Because I don't want you looking into the windows of my soul." A little later, forgetting he still had them on, he felt dissed when Richard Horowitz looked over his shoulder while talking to him. This was not normal. Horowitz had hired Mike to play the trombone as part of a multicultural happening he was producing, which would end in a parade on Essaouira's town square, and would be directly followed by the world premiere of the newly mastered *Othello*. Horowitz was able to do all sorts of things, like conducting orchestras and writing film scores, and he did it all well with neither complexes nor a need for chemicals. The expression "natural high" fit.

A specialist in North African music, Horowitz was creative, decisive, and communicative. He could delegate authority. He was confident of the value of his own talent. His good mental health began to assume a larger-than-life dimension for Staccato, who, all of a sudden and against all his instincts, found himself envious. Why could he not be more like Horowitz? This was pure paranoia. He was on a natural low, loaded with useless regrets. He grew increasingly jealous of Horowitz. The margin was suddenly not such a great place to be. This was Jealous City, remember. The gathering was all about the jealous Othello, who "threw away a pearl richer than all his tribe." Horowitz did whatever he had to do in order to do what he wanted to do. He had tuned pianos in Rabat for a living. After his Moroccan jazz fusion ensemble shared bills with the Kronos Quartet and David Byrne, he began to think that maybe he could find a way to have "one foot each in Christian and Muslim music." Trying to "add another dimension to what's already there," Horowitz "force fed" himself the technology necessary to try it. He accepted electronic music reluctantly. Feeling a bit guilty about deserting the acoustic camp, he was encouraged reading an essay by the composer Henry Cowell, which said that the tendency to update ethnic elements was "obviously neo-primitive in its striving for vitality and simplicity. It is not an attempt to imitate primitive music but rather to draw on those materials common to peoples of the world to build new music particularly related to their own century."

Paul Bowles, who had studied musical composition with Cowell, was also a novelist who wrote, for one, *The Sheltering Sky.* Living in Tangier, and having heard Horowitz's East/West fusion work, he recommended Horowitz to Bernardo Bertolucci, who was making a movie of *The Sheltering Sky.* It was an impressive credit, and Horowitz could command a large enough budget in Essaouira to engage two-count-'em-two trombones to play in the tribune. The money people were giving him the benefit of the doubt. They assumed Horowitz had good reasons to want two trombones to accompany the Daqqas and Gnawas he'd gone to so much trouble and expense to round up. He asked Staccato to hire the second one, and Staccato picked up Stanley, a lean, lanky, soft-spoken young African-American trombonist of Nob Hill buppie descent who had been working with African bands in Paris. African bands were loud. Horowitz had made it clear that he wanted two *loud* trombones. Thanks to Horowitz's budgetary benefit of the doubt, Johnny and Stanley were earning fortissimo fees to be paid in cash, tax-free, expenses paid—plus miscellaneous freebies and five-star perks. It should have been a dream trip.

Stanley was slow-moving, patient, with a thin face that was difficult to read. He played his cards close to his vest. He wore vests. Any eventual visual commitment was hesitant and limited. Stanley was either a deep thinker, a liar, or retarded. It was a black face that spoke with a white accent. Stanley would not look Staccato in the eye either. Rainer Maria Rilke wrote: "And so I hold myself back and swallow the call-note of my dark sobbing. Ah, whom can we ever turn to in our need?" Staccato, who liked to quote Rilke, thought that he could always turn to fellow-bebopper Stanley in his hour of need. He thought wrong. It would soon be clear that he would just have to swallow his dark sobbing. Johnny grew grotesquely dependent on Stanley, who turned out to be far from a drug fan. Unrealistic as it may have been, he really needed this cat, or at least he needed the hipster he presumed him to be. Stanley would surely help to prevent the self-destruction of a fellow trombone player. That was the card Johnny would play when the crunch came. Stanley was his Berlin Wall. Staccato was praying for an airlift.

He knew there must be something wrong with the vibe he was projecting when, out of nowhere, Stanley put his hands on his shoulders, and reassured him: "Don't worry, man. Everything is going to be okay." He talked to him like to a kid. *Merde alors.* He had not thought it was that serious. It was pathetic—everywhere that Stanley went Johnny followed. Call him Mr. Pitiful. He and his habit were no longer a loving couple. Stanley was the only person who could rescue his coming panic. Could this really be the end?

It was not Staccato's first drug panic. Like the other three—on the beach in Cannes, one cold day in Gstadt, a Sunday morning in August on an empty street in Paris—it took place under a bright sun. Bright sunshine terrified him. It was so temporary. Shaped like a big doughnut, the modern motel where the *Othello* people were staying was located between the blue sea and Essaouira's old ramparts. It enclosed a large dark green lawn and a swimming pool. The Moroccan sky was cloudless and the morning sun was already warm on the day when Stanley, Horowitz, Dennis Hopper, and some of the others went to visit the nearby hippie beach where Jimi Hendrix had written "Castles Made of Sand." Staccato chose to stay in his room and get stoned in peace.

Standing at his window looking at the pool, and the running, jumping, and splashing tourists around it, he wished he could run, jump, and splash like them. No, not really—it was like wishing to be more like Richard Horowitz. A passing cloud. Any territory at all was looking greener than the sorry, diseased knoll he was stranded on. The tourists may have been bourgeois, and not very pretty, but at least they didn't have the plague. Worst of all, he had infected himself by choice. He couldn't even blame God. Being jealous of people because they're sober is not a sign of a healthy spirit. He had lost the freedom to be sober. As with freedom, you don't realize how valuable sobriety is until you've lost it.

Being paid to come to an interesting, romantic, not yet touristy, and sunny old port like Essaouira to do things you like to do for free anyway is one of the few good reasons to become a musician or a writer in the first place. Hanging out with Dennis Hopper was better than being in the steel business. In Staccato's place, Mike would have been giving thanks. There was plenty to be thankful for. He did not have a backache, a toothache, cancer, or an unpleasant job. And he did have enough of that good old-fashioned medicated goo to cope with any unexpected sobering experiences. However, as when Jim Carrey's rowboat bangs into the dome he had not known he was living under in *The Truman Show*, Staccato was up against the limits of his own existence.

The massive musical street happening with large bands of Daqqas and Gnawas and two trombones began when Horowitz played his ney flute up by the cupola at twilight. He had hung on to his collection of flutes, even though he had not needed them during his electric fusion period: "Like lifeboats in a sea of technology." We deserve any lifeboat we can get. Outlined against the sky, ney in the air, Horowitz resembled a bird of prey. Daqqas with long nifars played an accelerating series of G naturals in front of the mosque while, from a small arcade, the trombones began to accompany the Gnawa percussionists on the hillside below. Flapping his arms, marshalling his multiethnic formations for the march, Horowitz motioned for the Gnawas to light their torches, for the Daqqas to play faster, and for the trombones to blow louder. Mike and Stanley blasted pedal tones, arpeggios, scales, and they counterslid between the first and seventh positions. They played tailgate smears, and rhythm and blues licks. It was hard work. With total concentration, using every bit of air he had, Staccato made sure to breathe correctly—pushing his stomach out while breathing in, pulling it in while blowing out. He was careful not to cut off circulation by pressing the mouthpiece too hard to his lips. He and Stanley made eye contact as they played contrapuntal lines (they were both wearing shades). Their complicity was penetrating. Music had done it again. Johnny was astonished by his discipline, power, and endurance, and by the joy of making music. Robert Crumb once said: "Music self-played is happiness self-made." Blowing a trombone can clean out your system, and, if your heart is in the right place, your mind.

So it would come to pass that the under-deep-cover double agent Johnny Staccato came in from the cold. A little late, perhaps, but three cheers for the kid. Methadone worked well enough for a while—it was a bit like being in the witness protection program. Methadone is the Manischewitz wine of drugs—a cheap high, acceptable only if you have no other choice. Methadone had less to do with Staccato coming in from the cold than his heroin dealer Ricky Cheval moving back to Montreal. Scoring from unreliable junkies in dodgy Parisian neighborhoods was demanding work. Staccato vaguely remembered Mike boasting that he did not need any material thing badly enough to stand in line for it. Methadone appeared to be a reasonable way to postpone the decision. The bad feeling you know is better than the good feeling you've forgotten.

When Johnny Staccato became an inactive drug fan, he died. Mike was back at the helm. The problem was that Mike's definition of sobriety included cannabis. We get the sobriety we deserve. As he aged, the Fabulous Furry Freak Brother maxim "dope will get you through times of no money better than money will get you through times of no dope" ("dope" meaning weed, in this case) became obvious rather than comic to him. Mike's friends Bob the film director and Momo the publisher had both gone into hyper-viper phases in their sixties. Neither one of them made a secret of being as stoned as possible as often as possible. They smoked all day long, no matter where they were or whom they were with. The septuagenarian composer Gil carried his pot pipe in his pocket, and smoked it openly in clubs and restaurants and on gigs. The constant high was sometimes inconvenient. On the band bus once, some of his musicians asked for advances and he casually passed out twenty-dollar bills. His disbelieving manager said: "Gil, you might want to think about getting receipts." Bob the filmmaker considered the cannabis high an unmixed blessing. He had been an aggressive drunk, and was having trouble getting work in Hollywood. When he stopped drinking and started to smoke, he became more tolerant, reliable, and imaginative. His career revived, and he made better movies, and more money. This is beginning to sound like a Viagra commercial. When strangers asked Momo what he did in life, he'd say: "I publish dirty books." Momo published envelope-stretching books that were banned in England and America, in English in France. He also published just plain dirty books. It was not so much that Momo began to smoke cannabis, but that he began never to not smoke it. Nothing—but nothing—he did sober was not better stoned. Momo figured that being able to stay stoned on hashish all day long was a sort of privilege of age, like a senior citizen discount. Oliver Saks said that one reason the years seem to fly by faster as we get older is that each year represents a smaller percentage of our lives. Seniors like to smoke weed because it slows them down. Middle-aged people who enjoyed smoking when they were younger sometimes find that grass makes them paranoid. The good news is that you can break through to the other side, where paranoia gives way to more pleasure than ever. Old folks can fix their heads if not their bodies.

When Mike was a young man, he was misinformed by grown-ups about marijuana. He assumed that their warnings about cocaine and heroin were also unreliable. A poor assumption. But it is also a mistake to think that all marijuana smokers are too wasted to run their lives properly. Drug czars' lies about the devil's weed are like saying all beer drinkers are drunken bums. The majority of people who smoke grass pay their bills, get to work on time, keep up with the news, and love their children; some of them vote Republican. We don't hear too much about normal people who smoke weed because if they are reasonably prudent, they don't get caught.

In his book *Saying Yes,* Jacob Sullum writes about a housewife who liked to snort heroin when she vacuumed the house. He cites a study that included interviews with sixty-one controlled opiate users. One subject was a forty-one-year-old carpenter who had used heroin on weekends for a decade. Married sixteen years, he lived with his wife and three children in the suburbs. Another was a twenty-seven-year-old college student who had used it two or three times a month for three years, then once a week for a year. A twenty-three-year-old graduate student said being on heroin was like "taking a vacation from yourself. When things get to you, it's a way of getting away without getting away."

If Kurt Cobain is to be believed, what the guy with the alternative vacation plans was really doing was saying "fuck it" every time he got bored. He was probably in for trouble. But maybe more people than we know can just say "fuck it" on the weekends (including a wake-up taste for Monday morning, it goes without saying).

Drug fans, active and inactive, talking about drugs are like baseball fans. It's the default conversation—what they talk about when they have nothing more urgent to say. In fact, it just may be that, when it gets right down to the nitty-gritty, and you are looking for closure, dude, when the fat lady sings at the end of the day, the bottom line will be that the best thing about drugs is talking about them.

When Mike asked Dizzy Gillespie if an ugly personality could make beautiful music, Dizzy eyeballed him and drawled: "Staaan Getz. Stan is a guy everybody thinks is nasty and yet he plays such sweet melodies. There has to be some tenderness in him somewhere. I told his wife: 'You ought to talk to Stan. People are saying negative things about him.' She said: 'Why don't you speak up for him? You're his friend.' So I said: 'Okay, tell me something nice to say about the son of a bitch.'"

18

THE INTERNATIONAL HERALD TROMBONE

I AM A FREE PERSON WHO IS DIFFICULT TO MANIPULATE.
WHAT MORE CAN I ASK FOR?
—VACLAV HAVEL

Who needs these garlic-chewing, truffle-nosed, cheese-eating surrender monkeys with their dumb thirty-five-hour work week and
seven weeks' paid vacation?

When the *New York Times* bought out its fifty percent partner the
Washington Post, word got around that the *International Herald Tribune* could be more efficiently run from Brussels or London, where
everybody spoke English and there were lower social costs. Better
yet, it could all be done from New York, which has even lower social costs than London or Brussels, and where the *Times* would soon
have plenty of room in its own skyscraper.

Paris, like the French language, was becoming expendable.

The quirky marriage between the *Times* and the *Post* in Paris had
somehow brought out the best in both of them. For a long time, the
Trib was called the best English-language paper in the world. Without the *Post,* the *Trib* had been slowly fading out of focus for years,
a decline punctuated by the cancellation of all complimentary sub-

scriptions. A daring cost-cutting move—you've got to give them credit. The deed came down without warning. Mike felt pretty silly calling the circulation department to complain about not getting his paper, and being told his comp had been eighty-sixed.

Then they cut back on freelancers. After running weekly for more than twenty years, Mike's column would now be biweekly. He was informed about it by a phone call from the editor, who didn't have much time to talk because he was running out to catch an airplane (probably flying first-class). These people were all heart. This whole story is a graduate course in insensitivity.

Then again, you have to remember that editors who survive downsizing tend to be overworked, stressed out, and touchy, with short fuses. Even in normal times, editors relate to freelance writers like the scorpion to the frog. They sting—it's their nature. Editors are jealous of freelancers because, to begin with they do not have to come into the office every day. Cutting a few freelancers by 50 percent saved the *Trib* the kind of figure the balance sheet treats as lunch money. Mike had no contract, but he wasn't complaining. He was in the margin, after all, by choice.

Also called a peg, a hook in a daily paper can be defined as something unusual that happened yesterday, or will happen tomorrow. At the limit, last week or next. A taste of sex, drugs, and violence helps. Round-numbered anniversaries of births or deaths are great hooks. No romantic modulations or fanciful tangents writing them up, please. Journalism squashes writers into shortcuts and cul de sacs; into the world of the eight-hundred-word article. "Are (were) you nervous about playing Carnegie Hall for the first time?" is a good hook. Questions regarding the narrowest possible definition of the subject are central to a hook: "How does it feel to have a hit record? . . . Is it true that you've been out with Nicole?"

When Mike interviewed Raed El-Khazen, a Lebanese guitar player, in New York in October 2001, one month after 9/11, the hook was based on instinct, not experience. The concept of a hook had never been important to him. Dan Wolf at the *Voice* had told him not to worry about news. "Make your own news," he said. Raed was just an obviously good story. Marcel, now a professional bass guitar player living in Brooklyn, had befriended Raed when they were students at the Berklee College of Music. Raed's ambition was to be a working jazz musician, not easy at best. His name was more than merely inconvenient in New York at the time, and his student visa had expired.

El-Khazen had grown up amidst explosions, snipers, and general chaos in Beirut. He was grateful to America for having allowed him the freedom to choose what he wanted to do with his life. But he had left Beirut to get away from the rack and the ruin, and now, in New York, he found himself in the middle of it again. "The karma is not so good in New York right now," he said. "Not that it was any better in Beirut." He was wearing a week's stubble on his brown face, and wraparound shades, and his dark curly hair was wild and wooly. When Mike asked him how it was these days in New York for somebody who looked like him, he replied: "Not so bad. People think I'm an Israeli."

Mike's El-Khazen story ran in the *Trib* in November 2001, when Ground Zero was still on front pages. His editor called him to say there had been complaints from upstairs that the article had no hook. No new album, no concert tour, no Victoria's Secret ad, no foundation grant, no drug bust. Mike apologized, and promised to be more careful in the future. After hanging up, he kicked himself. The right response should have been "That's not true." A freaky Arab jazz guitar player who left Beirut for the peace and quiet of America living in post-9/11 New York was not too bad a hook. Mike had become so accustomed to being reduced to his narrowest possible definition that the big picture was blurred. His territory was not uninteresting, but it was far removed from Ground Zero. His editors could not imagine an article by their jazz critic as being relevant to any definition of a major hook, and so they concluded that there was no hook at all. Mike almost called back to complain, but in the end, he beat his habitual strategic retreat into the holes of the Swiss cheese, where he discovered . . .

. . . Aziza Mustafa Zadeh, who had been described as "beautiful enough to sink a thousand ships." Billed as the "Oriental Princess of Jazz," she spoke Azeri, Georgian, Russian, English, and German. Her father, Vagif Mustafa Zadeh, had been the best jazz pianist in Azerbaijan at a time when such nationality and occupation were not exactly paths to success in the Soviet Union. A cult hero to the sort of people who listened to the Voice of America, he became a legend after he died of a heart attack while performing onstage. Aziza had performed with her father since the age of three. They combined jazz feeling with folk songs when that sort of thing was subversive. People stood up and screamed and broke chairs during concerts. After studying piano at the Baku conservatory, she began to write songs and sing them. She sang standards "in my own way. Not the standard way. We must each find our own face."

They were in the bar of a Holiday Inn in Paris next to the *periferique* during happy hour. Her mellifluous voice was getting lost in the rush-hour buzz.

"Sorry—find our own what?"

"Fate," she said this time. It had been her fate to be living in Mainz, Germany, which was twinned with Baku. She felt comfortable there because people in Mainz were "thinking in a way I really like."

"What kind of way is that?"

"If you will know me better you will not ask such questions. Will you please put out that cigarette? I will have an attack. If I was president of the world, I would order no more smoking."

"You sound as though you like to give orders."

"I just try and follow nature."

"Sorry—follow what?"

"You know, I can read you. I can read people like a book. I know exactly what you are trying to do. How do you say it?—back me into a corner. Smoking is bad for the air and the leaves. I am sorry to speak so loud. You should try to look beyond words and pay attention to eyes. Words cannot tell you anything deep anyway. Try to understand intonation and aura. Did you know, for example, that you can learn a lot about people from the personalities of their pet animals?"

"Do you have a pet?"

"Yes, a cat."

"I'm allergic to cats."

"I knew it. I told you, I can read you."

Her mother, a veteran hoofer, was chaperoning Aziza on this tour. "She really can read people," her mother said. Aziza hugged her, and added: "Show business is in my blood. I never get nervous before going onstage because the stage is home to me."

"Jacques Brel used to throw up before going onstage."

"Who?"

"Jacques Brel, a Belgian singer."

"Why should I know about him? Does he know about me?"

"He died."

"That does not matter. Energy never goes away. Death is only biological. The spirit continues. I still talk to my father."

"Does he talk back?"

"Of course. It's a dialogue. I ask him what to do when I don't know the way and he helps me. If somebody hurts me, that person gets punished one way or another. Do not worry. I will speak in your favor."

"Sorry—speak in my what?"

With the benefit of hindsight, an unknown Azeri jazz singer was probably not worth eight hundred words in the best English-language newspaper in the world. A journalist with the freedom to publish such an eccentric little story on such a marginal subject in a mass-circulation daily paper was highly unusual. Aziza was a hole in the Swiss cheese.

The editors were trying so hard to keep their eye on the ball that they didn't see Mike sliding headfirst into second base. The *International Herald Tribune* was being invaded like some nineteenth province by the *New York Times*. The attitude was, roughly, *you are either with us or against us. We take no prisoners. Times* editor Howell Raines, who will be known here under the more ecological spelling of Howl Reigns, was a flaunter of unilateral power worthy of Donald Rumsfeld. Reigns and his junta were apparently not very nice people.

From the statement of resignation by the chairman and CEO of the *International Herald Tribune,* Peter C. Goldmark Jr.: "The end of the IHT as an independent newspaper, with its own voice and its own international outlook, is a great loss. The world needs more independent voices, not fewer." He went on to say: "I was not quite ready to go, but the New York Times has asked me to go. There is a code in the corporate world. Under that code you are expected to leave it murky as to whether you are resigning or being fired; you are supposed to go quietly; you are supposed to say everything is OK; and you often pick up a nice fat check at the door. But this is a time when the world is growing to mistrust America; it needs thoughtful voices and independent perspectives that see the world whole and are not managed from America. On this and other issues of importance to me the New York Times and I did not see eye to eye, so I am going to break that code today. Believe me, I will pay dearly for this, both financially and in other coin."

Without the *Washington Post* in the mix, there began to be less depth, less quirkiness, less "attitude" in the *Trib*. The quality of the new color photo technology seemed to be getting more attention than the black and white words between them. Mike was advised to be happy to be writing for the *New York Times* because it was something most journalists would kill for. Of course this wasn't the *real New York Times,* but it was as close as he was likely to get. It puzzled him that there had been no notification of a change of ownership—no welcome wagon, no "happy to have you aboard," no "Thank you, Masked Man." His column was a given, taken for granted, like the bridge column. Bridge columnists should not expect a "Thank you, Masked Man." After the purchase was officially announced, Mike asked his editor if he should continue to send in his column as usual, and the reply was: "Far as I know."

"Far as I know" would have made a good mantra for the early twenty-first-century *Trib*. You could sense the fear and the loathing in the office over the telephone. There was a rumor that *New York Times* editors would be coming to take over, although nobody seemed to know exactly what that meant. Far as Mike knew, each article would be his last. No respected veteran journalist should have to accept such an insecure professional situation . . .

But fuck that professional journalism shit. Charlie Parker played every solo as though it would be his last, and we have been told that insecurity is the fountain of youth. You can get stuck in the role that other people fit you into: "Him? Oh, he's a journalist." At heart, Mike was always a musician. There was a suggestion that this book be called *The International Herald Trombone,* which has a nice musical ring to it. And which brings us back to Miles Davis. Everything brings us back to Miles Davis.

Tony Williams, who joined Miles when he was seventeen, knew musicians who were "as crazy as loons who made beautiful music." He knew bands the members of which hated one another that made beautiful music together. Music transcends such things. He was twelve the first time he played the drums in public—the first time he ever touched a kit. As his technique got better, he began to suspect that the drums were more important than he was. He wanted to make the drums the most beautiful instrument in the world, as romantic as violins and as heroic as trumpets. He compared the learning process to a dusty living room. You are comfortable there. It's home. But one day you see something in a corner that attracts your attention. You never saw it before. To get to it, you have to move everything and clean the dust. He cleaned and cleaned, and eventually he found this very beautiful vase. Improvising is about being able to clean the dust, to find your vase, and recognize that it is beautiful. He firmly believed that whatever you want, you can make it happen. Williams was one of those short men who managed to tower over you. He left Miles to make his own music with his jazz-rock fusion band Lifetime, and the lesson he learned when it failed was: "People are not necessarily affected by excellence." He chalked Lifetime's lack of success up to the "stylistic fascists on the jazz scene who deal in fear—who tell people that this or that music is dangerous. There's a clique in New York who are trying to rewrite history. It's a marketing gambit. They don't even play that well, they just know how to walk and talk a certain way. They go around telling people what to listen to and not listen to. Miles was never like that. You know, I never really recovered from his death. It was tough for me to live in a world without Miles. When I was thirteen, Miles was already teaching kids like me about self-esteem, to fight for our rights. That was his real importance, as much as the music. He was saying those things before Rosa Parks got on the bus, before Martin Luther King. When some cops beat him up in front of Birdland — when was it, 1959? — he took them to court and won the case. He carried himself like he was king of the world. Miles was the point man. In the army, the scouts go out, and there's always one guy twenty or thirty yards up ahead who makes sure the coast is clear. Then he waves to the other guys that it's safe to move up. Miles was the point man who took all the heat. There are no more point men."

About the same time, Joe Henderson told Mike that he felt as though *he* was "on the point. The first shot gets fired, I get hit. The point man is expendable." Henderson's wise and gentle smile had just appeared on the cover of *Down Beat* magazine. It was a "look who's still around" kind of article. Bird lives. Glenn Miller has been playing "In the Mood" in the Roseland Ballroom all these years. Elvis is still singing "Jailhouse Rock" in Las Vegas. Supposedly toast, Henderson was discovered in the flesh living in San Francisco. He had been the tenorman of the hour for years. He questioned not past absence but current presence: "Being on a *Down Beat* cover doesn't make any difference to me in terms of what I'm trying to do out here. I've been doing it for thirty years."

Henderson's comeback had been started by his album *Lush Life*, the first under his own name in eleven years. It was on the charts for months. He had not wanted to "go into a studio and just make another record. I didn't have anything new to say. It took me eleven years to get some ideas buzzing around in my brain." The most obvious and immediate change in Henderson's life on the road involved a big improvement in the nature of his hotel rooms. He was "happy to be able to walk around the bed without tripping on my suitcase. I'm the last one to have an opinion of what I deserve or don't deserve. You can't please everyone. We can only convince them that perhaps we are a bit more valuable than they considered us. I just try to get from sunup to sundown with as much dignity as possible." But he was puzzled. You are *supposed* to play well.

That's what it's all about—playing well. It's the whole point. Why was everybody suddenly praising him for it?

"I got into the music business because it was fun," said the saxophonist and arranger Don Menza, announcing his retirement. "Now I've become concerned with where it's been going. I used to enjoy the challenge of being able to go out and create all this music, but the record business is becoming more concerned about how we look than how we sound."

And it was true that being a good-looking young woman was a big help in the world of jazz. "Looking good is half of it," Miles said (everything comes back to Miles Davis). Records by female jazz singers were flooding Mike's in-box, most wrapped in packages promoting cleavage, bare limbs, pretty faces, and malfunctionable wardrobes. Some could sing, most not. The great number of jazz recordings by sexy women reflected the increasing emphasis on youth and skin-deep beauty in American culture, where vapidity was mistaken for minimalism.

Some critics have said something like that about Norah Jones, but it's not true in her case. That such good taste could still sell multimillions of units was welcome news. Jones's music would work well in elevators, although you might be reluctant to get off. Simple but far from dumb, laid-back with a reassuring groove, country edges, and sustained organ and guitar chords, it was just the ticket for the age of chaos and woe. In contrast to the vulgarity of her fellow superstar singer-songwriter Janet Jackson, with her Super Bowl wardrobe malfunction. There could be no wardrobe malfunctions in jazz. Some suit-clad conservatives excepted there were no wardrobes in jazz. Were it more vulgar, jazz music might be more successful. Vulgarity was just not an option. Try to think of one vulgar jazzman—Kenny G comes to mind, and there are certainly others, but not many. There have been insensitive and un-swinging jazzmen, and the music has been *presented* with vulgarity, but that's not the music's fault. Jazz was music not show business. Show business was based on lies. Jazz was the truth. Lying was vulgar. Marketing an album by a pneumatic, underclothed young woman with nothing much to say as a jazz record is a lie.

Speaking of lying about jazz, Bill Clinton revealed the contents of his iPod to *Down Beat:* "Most of the Gil Evans/Miles Davis lexicon, Stan Getz's early fifties recordings, Ella Fitzgerald and Louis Armstrong, much Coltrane, seven versions of "Summertime" and six versions of "Body and Soul." *Down Beat* quoted Clinton: "I want to hear if somebody can play 'Body and Soul' in a way I find more interesting than Coleman Hawkins did it." A bit too esoteric to be true; could such programming have been possible without the help of a spinner or two? Early fifties Getz, indeed. Although there was no good reason why he should bother to lie about such a thing, at the same time, you could not help wondering what Clinton said was on his iPod when he talked to *Rolling Stone.*

"It's a pleasure to be back here," Getz told an audience in Copenhagen, not long before he died. He already knew he was dying. "This is déjà vu for me. I lived in Copenhagen for three years. I left my heart in Copenhagen." The audience sighed with satisfaction and applauded, before Getz chuckled and added: "I said the same thing last night in Stockholm." Was that a lie? Was he playing with their heads? It could have gone either way. He had lived in both cities. Ambiguity is to jazz what vulgarity is to show business—not necessary but welcome.

Getz rented a seaside villa in Saint-Jean Cap Ferrat, on the French Riviera, where he lived as though he were writing the screenplay, playing the hero, and orchestrating a soundtrack for a movie about his own death. He had liver cancer and a dark sense of humor. Getz, who changed women as often as he changed musical styles, was in love with his current girlfriend. When she was not in the room, he played his horn to her empty chair. He had finally found his girl from Ipanema. He changed personas almost as often. Getz the monster was his most famous persona. Many of those who complained about Getz being so evil had in fact failed one of the tests he liked to lay on people. He was always raising the emotional stakes, and he had no patience with those who would not ante up. The announcement in Copenhagen had been a test. Since the audience laughed, they passed, so he played like a monster that night.

He liked to play Iago, the evil one; he recited passages from *Macbeth*. You could never be sure where the role stopped and reality began. It was as though he was saying, *You say I'm a monster? If you can't see any deeper than that, that's your problem. Go read Shakespeare.*

Suddenly it became no longer a game but sudden death. Once he was aware of his terminal condition, after a decade or so of relative mediocrity, his saxophone playing grew noticeably more muscular and creative, and less sentimental. The monster had an angelic side.

"It was impossible to make such tender music and be *only* a monster," his friend and photographer Jean-Pierre Larcher said. "Stan considered his life less important than what his imagination could make of it."

Getz went to great lengths to create and promote his own legend, although the plot thickened by itself. In the middle of a take while recording a song called "Her" with Eddie Sauter for the album *Focus*, Getz was called away to take a phone call informing him about the death of his mother. He came back, picked up the headphones, and continued to record "Her," but on a deeper level. When Sauter was writing the soundtrack for Arthur Penn's film *Mickey One*, Penn suggested Getz for the solos. The director soon saw that Warren Beatty's character had certain parallels to Getz. They were both taking drugs and burning themselves out with women. Both were still searching for beauty in their own way. Penn wanted the music to bridge the gap between this man's happy past and threatening present. It was essential to the film.

"Stan got it right away," Larcher said. "He was a sensitive person who could become ill when confronted with human misery. It was physical, not intellectual. He vomited seeing a homeless wino on a cold night on Delancey Street. He found a kind of fugitive peace through the creation of beautiful music. Whether he succeeded or not was very important to him. When he felt he had played the right phrase with the most beautiful notes possible, he was reassured in the face of his own death."

Getz could be slick and sentimental—it was part of what had made him so very popular. It was his biggest flaw, and he knew it: "He wanted people to cry when he played a ballad," Larcher continued. "It is difficult to show so much emotion without flirting with mawkishness. Everybody wants to play beautifully. Getz wanted more; he wanted to be emotionally profound." Antonio Carlos Jobim said that "beauty is subversive," and Getz's monstrous side was never gone for long. He manipulated people—his family, musicians, his manager, his women—through his combination of beauty and violence. It was the violence that produced the beauty.

When *Rolling Stone* asked the then presidential candidate Bill Clinton what music he'd like to have at his inaugural ball, he replied: "Too bad Stan Getz is dead." Maybe he programmed his own iPod, after all.

Meanwhile, the situation at the *International Herald Trombone* was coming to an inevitable worst-case scenario. Or so it seemed at the time. Mike was not introduced to, and there were neither complaints nor compliments from, the new people running the paper. Months and years went by. Whatever office news he heard was through the grapevine. When asked about the corporate infighting, *Trib* editors would clam up like mobsters being asked to rat on the Mafia. He just knew there was a whole bunch of unholy shit happening.

The good news was that Howl Reigns had to leave the *New York Times* after his protégé Jayson Blair was caught making up and stealing stuff for articles, and it came out how unpopular his howling and reigning had made him. Later he was published by the *Guardian*, an English newspaper, where he was now free to be an independent voice and criticize American journalism. He quoted an article by Richard Reeves that compared Gerald Ford to Bozo the Clown. "The rules of conventional journalism," Reeves wrote, "make it almost impossible to report that a presidential candidate 'had nothing to say and said it badly to a stunned crowd.' Big news organizations are captives of our own rules of fairness. Voters are doubly disadvantaged—by a paucity of information in the campaign coverage, and by the elusive nature of the evidence about the kinds of intelligence that matter in our leaders." Reigns was replaced at the *Times* by Bill Keller, who had treated Mike as family when he had been the *Times*'s Moscow correspondent, and Mike had passed through on his way back from the Siberian jazz festival. The kindness had been a nice surprise. Mike hoped it would not hurt Keller's career.

Mainly, though, Mike was hoping that his byline would endure through at least one more jazz festival season.

VIENNE, France—When twenty-one teenage music students from the Ukrainian mining town of Krivoj Rog perform in France and play Cannonball Adderley's R&B hit "Mercy, Mercy, Mercy," which was written by Joe Zawinul, an Austrian, it can be said that jazz is world music.

AGADIR, Morocco—Trying to preserve centuries-long West African ethnic musical traditions on a giant outdoor stage wired with a sound system worthy of Led Zeppelin, located not far from a Club Med, and between a McDonalds, a Pizza Hut and the Sheraton hotel, is, as Lenny Bruce said in another context, a "big gig."

SIENA, Italy—The 33rd Siena Jazz Festival in late July and early August was sponsored by, among others, the town of Siena, the province of Siena, the region of Tuscany and the Monte Dei Paschi Di Siena bank, which was founded in 1472, before Columbus discovered bebop. A student saxophonist on the ramparts of the fourteenth-century Fortezza Medicea was practicing Charlie Parker's "Billie's Bounce," which was written before *Time* magazine discovered Thelonious Monk. Tradition is alive and well in Italy.

Reviewing jazz festivals does not enter into our scheme here. With lede graphs like that, who needs reviews anyway? Festival reviews require the lowest common denominator hooks available. What was played, when, by whom, and was it too fast, too slow, or in or out of tune. It takes some serious sniffing around to find the holes in the Swiss cheese at festivals, which are constructed precisely to be all cheese. Whatever that means.

The San Sebastian (Donostia in Basque) Jazz Festival in the Spanish Basque Country checked Mike into the five-star Maria Cristina hotel. There was a view of the Bay of Biscay, and it was so luxurious that the needles in the sewing kits were pre-threaded. Mike imagined little old Basque ladies threading sewing needles in the basement. Over kippers in the Maria Cristina's Edwardian breakfast room, he struck up a conversation with Charles Lloyd, who would perform that night. Lloyd was talking about his recently deceased drummer Billy Higgins, and one passing led to another. Mike told Lloyd that he had discovered that their late mutual friend Michel Petrucciani was buried next to Frédéric Chopin in Père-Lachaise cemetery. It was an expensive piece of real estate, but Michel never did take up much space.

Petrucciani had, at different times, pulled both of them out of early musical retirement. Suffering from osteogenesis imperfecta, also known as "glass bones," Michel was tiny and fragile. He needed to be carried. Mike and Lloyd had each carried the little French prodigy in their arms when he was a teenager. As a preteen, a prisoner of his deformity, Michel had had nothing better to do than sit at the keyboard and practice all day long. With his enormous gift, he became a monster piano player early in life. Michel was also carried by Kenny Clarke, Clark Terry, Sugar Blue, and Lee Konitz. There was some talk about forming a Michel Carrier Club. Somehow, carriers were always available. How bemused Michel looked being carried in grown men's arms. Raising his eyebrows behind oversized black-rimmed glasses, he seemed to be asking, *Do you believe this weird shit that happened to me?*

Mike first met him on a midsummer's night on the unpaved main street of the Provençal village of Cliuscat, when, wearing a Count Basie–style yachting cap, a tiny hipster leaned out of one of those sardine-can Citroen 2CVs and shouted: "Hey, baby." At the age of fifteen, they were the only English words Michel knew. He learned "motherfucker," "cunt," and "asshole" before the rest of it. Musicians were beginning to talk about this little cat of Corsican descent who lived in Montelimar and played like he was from New York.

Montelimar was just north of the French California. The Petrucciani house was located between the autoroute and the railroad tracks—freight was constantly coming and going. His mother cooked sausages in the garden, his father and brother played guitar and bass. People came down from the hills from kilometers around to sit by the fire and eat and blow and listen to music. Mike, who had been watching the grapes and the cherries grow in Les Grands Cléments, drove up to play with Michel—trying to seduce mistress music one more time. Michel had outsized desire, emotion, and chops. He was totally in the moment, and improvising with him was liberating. There was no such thing as a mistake.

The owner of a café halfway up to the ruined chateau of the Marquis de Sade on the top of the hilly Vauclusian village of Lacoste approached Mike to play a gig on his terrace. Mike and Michel decided to do it as a duo. They went over to set it up together.

"What kind of jazz do you play?" the owner asked, his Bic poised over a pad of cross-section paper. Mike and Michel looked at each other. Nothing exciting came to mind. "Modern jazz" and "bebop" were two possibilities.

The owner raised his pen in the air with the idea: *"Le bon jazz d'après guerre."* Good postwar jazz. What war? It did not matter. Mike and Michel smiled. That was exactly the kind of jazz they played.

Eventually, Michel went off to the American California, where he dropped in unknown and unannounced on Lloyd, who had been more or less meditating full-time in Big Sur. Michel introduced himself, and told the lanky and bemused saxophone player that he was one of his heroes and he wanted to make music with him. Lloyd took this twisted little angel showing up at his door out of the blue begging to make music with him to be a sign from the gods.

Michel grew sturdier in his twenties—he no longer required carriers. Seeing that small body with the laughing face shuffle onstage with crutches was a sight anybody who had seen it did not soon forget. Dwarfed by the concert grand, he was a tiny presence writ large. His short legs required a custom-built extension to reach the piano pedals, but his hands could easily span a tenth. It was said that his penis matched his hand genes. With his wildly ironic sense of humor, including about himself, when he said that he would probably not last long, it was somehow not taken seriously. It was inspiring, how much he loved life—though his Napoleon impression could be a downer. He drank wine, took drugs, wives, and mistresses, and he had several children. His son inherited the glass bones disease. Michel saw himself as a sort of gangster of love. He was a relentless flirt. When a woman he was splitting a taxicab with asked him to stop feeling her breasts, he flashed his seductive smile, spread his palms innocently, and said: "Hey, baby, it's only me." Little old crippled harmless me. Ain't I cute? Then he put his hand up her skirt. The way his music combined soul with technique, commerciality with purity, and humor with gravitas, Michel could get away with a lot on many levels. Physically, though, he was pushing it, and he would pay. He was lucky to reach the age of thirty-six.

Michel was a personification of the victory of the spirit over the flesh. An incarnation of Dostoyevsky's "idiot," the "wholly beautiful man" whose function it was to disseminate a new state of being. Knowing Michel led to a reevaluation of the definitions of ugliness and beauty, and of bad and good luck. Charles Lloyd called Michel Petrucciani an "avatar."

There were no more avatars. Joe Henderson and Miles Davis had passed. No more point men. The wait for the mainstream jazz tradition to reawaken risked being long. Not that the tradition was dead, only that the culture that produced it was moving on. Jazz was growing out not up—horizontally not vertically. It may or may not have been getting better, but it was definitely getting to more places.

The Istanbul Jazz Festival furnished journalists with student guides who took them to the concerts and around town. John, who was studying international law at Tufts, told Mike that he smoked like a Turk, and that he should not worry about his expanding stomach because, as the old Turkish saying goes: "A man without a belly is like a house without a balcony." From a good family, John was also diplomatic. He would probably be a minister one day. One thing he was not, though, was a jazz fan. He was at a loss listening to Burhan Ocal's suite *Groove a la Turca*, which included two DJs from Marseilles scratching and sampling over a Latin beat, while a large man named Habib, who carried heavy loads on the docks of Izmir for a living, belted Turkish folk songs like a stevedore. John considered the work to be a jazzing-up of Turkish culture. Ocal was combining Oriental raps with silky modal harmony, blue notes, jazz licks, and percussion, and odd meters accompanied a bubbling backbeat groove. Like anything really new, it was politically incorrect. It was also very loud, and, the future minister notwithstanding, the young Turks in the audience loved it.

Ocal had performed in Zurich, Berlin, and, with the Kronos String Quartet, in San Francisco, and with the Joe Zawinul Syndicate in Paris. He played to full houses on Anatolian tours. Born in a Thracian village, he was introduced to percussion by his father, and to religious vocal music by his mother. Having mastered scales and modes and percussion instruments while still a boy, he said it was "my good luck" to have grown up in a place where unorthodox rhythmic patterns were part of everyday life. He learned them like learning how to walk. When he played in some time signature like 45/16 he did not even have to count. Accompanying himself on a darbuka finger drum, he illustrated: eleven plus nine, and eleven again makes thirty one, and add a five, and finish with another nine. "See? It's easy," he said. Ocal was always the leader of any group he was in: "I am a natural leader. I am like Bruce Lee. You must be strong with musicians. Musicians are not easy. I love music. I love action. I can sleep in the streets like a Gypsy or I am also living the high life in five-star hotels. It is of no importance to me. When I went to a Turkish classical music conservatory I was bored after a few weeks. I went to a jazz academy in Switzerland, and that was boring too. I am not classical or folk or rock or jazz. I am only following my instincts."

Following their instincts, at least two generations of foreign music students came to America to study the rules of jazz and rock at the Berklee College of Music, or in a similar program elsewhere (there were hundreds). They learned the vocabulary, took it back home with them, and started their own jazz programs in cities such as Porto, Helsinki, Paris, Tel Aviv, Hanoi, and Trondheim. Enrico Rava did his Italian take on the opera *Carmen*. Ocal's mentor Okay Temiz led a band called the Black Sea Jazz Orchestra. Guitarist Nguyen Le combined jazz with Vietnamese music. There were jazz musicians in Kazakhstan.

Someday, the subtitle *The Story of America's Music* for a documentary called *Jazz* may no longer be appropriate. Not that the history would become "history"—forgotten. The foundation would remain while the superstructure evolved. Manfred Eicher of ECM Records described jazz as "music from the edge. And the edge moves to the center, where there are people with good antennas, and it becomes a new central fact." Tunisian oud player Anouar Brahem recorded with Dave Holland and John Surman for ECM. In Galicia, northwestern Spain, Carlos Nunez was playing traditional Galician music on Celtic bagpipes as if they were an electric guitar, and he was fusing it with the blues, flamenco, and Arabic and Gypsy music. "I love it when music is old and modern at the same time," he said.

Combining old and modern music is not easy to do, and it's anything but a sure thing. In the meantime, while there were no new point men, a jazz fan could go to just about any city in the developed world and hear a world-class rhythm section. Jazz was in the process of becoming the musica franca, spoken everywhere. It was cultural colonialism—neither good nor bad, but inevitable. Not unlike the English language.

Jazz was born in the early twentieth century from a marriage of European forms, harmony, and instruments with African rhythms. Adolphe Sax had invented the saxophone, which was cheaper to buy, easier to play, and projected better than strings. From Sidney Bechet, Coleman Hawkins, Lester Young, and Charlie Parker to John Coltrane, the saxophone family was in the frontline from the beginning. As intercultural communication became easier, roots became branches, and branches grew leaves that grew new roots. Randy Weston called African music "an enormous tree. It is our past as well as our future. African music is more present in our lives than ever. Blues, samba, calypso, reggae, salsa, jazz—Africa is everywhere."

Postwar jazz musicians were listening to recordings of Pygmy music from the Congo. The Brazilian samba, of African origin, combined with bebop, also of African origin, from New York, to make bossa nova. Galician bagpipers and Turkish percussionists were playing the blues. Cultural exclusivity was no longer possible. The title of the book *Jazz Away from Home* was becoming obsolete. "Home" itself was in the process of being redefined.

Being an expatriate was neither temporary nor a matter of choice for Lemmy Constantine. Having been named after a role his American father played in French movies created its own destiny. His father, Eddie, became known as "le Bogart Francais" by portraying the American private investigator Lemmy Caution in a series of popular French films (such as *Le Grand Bluff*) made from the crime books of Peter Cheyney, an Englishman. It added up to an American playing a Frenchman playing an American. With his craggy face and narrow-brim hats, Eddie Constantine came across as a sympathetic rogue, and there were roles in new-wave films by

Agnes Varda, Rainer Fassbinder, and Jean-Luc Godard (*Alphaville*). He played Sloth, a bored movie idol, in Godard's section of *Seven Deadly Sins*.

Lemmy (for Lemmuel) spoke English with French body language, traveled on an American passport, was mistaken for a Canadian, and called himself a "second-generation expat." That his album was only available on his Web site did not make him particularly unhappy. Despite looking hard, he'd found no distribution deal. Maybe it was better this way. Poetic songs with English lyrics set to a Manouche Gypsy swing groove must be heard in an international context to be appreciated. On the Web, at least he had international distribution. Theoretically, the album was available everywhere. Dealing with their e-mails, he got to know people who enjoyed his music. When he sold a CD, he deposited it at the post office in person—he might even deliver it. Now that the album was being played on the radio, and the band was getting club dates, he'd even come to enjoy hawking it. Proud to sell music he was proud of, he was glad of the excuse to call Charles Aznavour, a friend of his father's whom he knew as a child, to ask if his band could open for him for old times' sake.

Where were we?

Like the song that says there "is no yes in yesterday," there was no "too" in Mike's tomorrow. His career had come down to a photo finish with technology. It had led through a variety of technological minefields. When the fully integrated steel mills were stifling independent rebar fabricators like his family's Dome Steel, he resigned to play the trombone. It was a close call. A few years later, Dome went bankrupt. Then he was getting calls for well-paid studio work just as instrumentalists began to be synthesized down the electronic tubes. Luckily, he left the recording industry to become a journalist. New York daily papers were having labor trouble; there were regular strikes. The *Village Voice* would be the only paper in the kiosks. The *Trib*'s ancestor the venerable *New York Herald Tribune* tanked, as did the *World-Telegram*, and the *Journal-American*. The weekly *Voice* took off—writers were getting one raise after another. Mike spent three years as European editor. Fortunately he was fired before they started giving the *Voice* away for free in New York. In the *International Herald Tribune*—"by the time you pronounce it you've missed your plane," Art Buchwald said—Mike could be read in over two hundred countries and territories. He got e-mails from Cairo, Oslo, Nairobi, London, and Mumbai. International was Mike's first name. You'd think that writing in Paris about "America's classical music" and being read all over the world except in America would have been a dream come true for a hipster who took such pride in marginality. Maybe it was at that.

In an article in which Condoleeza Rice was described as "unusually intelligent," an official who wanted to remain anonymous was quoted: "Condi never has an opinion of her own. She only thinks about what's good for the president." Is that really intelligence? If you had to choose, would it be better to be intelligent or moral? Was intelligence without sensitivity better than the other way around? Were quick reflexes a sign of intelligence, or quickness? Intelligent people can be bigots. They can be arrogant. Richard Nixon, an intelligent man, said that he only lost his temper on purpose. Intelligent people can be co-opted. Mike thought the *Times* had been co-opted. Although co-opted by exactly whom or what, he was not quite sure. Luckily, it had nothing to do with him. He was in the margin.

Despite the skill and doggedness with which he maintained his straight-journalist cover, Mike always remained a musician at heart. You never retire from music. The colonel in the army is addressed as "Colonel" until the end of his life. Once a "Professor," always a professor. A doctor is always called "Doctor." Musicians, no matter what kind of music they play, deserve an up-front benefit of the doubt. In *Tropic of Cancer,* Henry Miller wrote: "I am thinking that when the great silence descends upon all and everywhere music will at last triumph." Something you cannot really say about journalism.

In the middle of such metaphysical twists and turns, Mike's grandnephew Loomis came from Tampa to visit his uncle in France. "Frayance," he pronounced it. Loomis, who was seventeen, told his mother he thought it was cool that his uncle played with a band called Birth of the Cool—and wasn't it awesome how he had found a way to live outside the system? Loomis had a few things to learn about the system. Having dropped out of high school, and doing little but smoke dope, staying out of it was more or less his major. Loomis was the only one among his friends who was being raised by biological parents living together. His friends were periodically tested with drug detection kits their parents purchased from Wal-Mart. Other than wishing he would do it less, Loomis's mother, Mike's niece Rebecca, did not really mind his smoking grass. The problem was that Loomis, who had a poster of Bob Marley smoking a giant spliff on the wall of his room, could not tell his friends she approved because they might tell their parents, and they would call the cops. Parents apparently did that sort of thing in Tampa. Who was the American who said "My country is all Midwest"? There was an item in the *Trib* about a student in a small town in the Midwest who was caught entering school carrying guns he intended to fire. The journalist called him an "oddball." Oddball is an odd word for so much alienation and aggression. In that great Midwest out there, and it includes Tampa, not going to church was enough to risk being called an oddball. Life was easier if you did not say anything negative about neoconservatism. Imagine a sensitive boy like Loomis growing up in the middle of such uptight American heartland lunacy with liberal parents who were alienated to begin with. His alienation showed when he refused to look at the Eiffel Tower and the Arch de Triomphe because everybody else was looking at them. He did not want to look like a tourist. Marginal Mike could identify with that—staying out of the system can be hard work. Loomis would have to learn that some things are interesting even though everybody else is interested in them. You could sense his basic sanity, though, by the way he saw everything he really needed to see out of the corners of his eyes. He was a model houseguest. He would eat anything, and whatever time was good for you was good for him. He cleaned up after himself, he never complained, and he was always happy to try and communicate. This was not his image at home— Rebecca was astonished to hear it. It's complicated being seventeen. Mike took Loomis to Craig and Marie-Celine's annual summer solstice chili party in their penthouse—the "Sky Ranch"—in the fancy suburb of Boulogne. Their wide terrace went around all four sides of their thirteen-story building. In back, it faced the Eiffel Tower, which loomed large in their eastern sky. It so happened that the blinking white lights that had been discontinued after the millennium passed were being turned on again, some years later, for the first time that night. The Eiffel Tower may seem campy to people who have never seen it, but once you do, it's got your respect. The guests were looking at their watches to make sure they remembered to run around back and not miss the light show on the hour. They were a mixture of French and American—journalists, Unesco employees, literary agents, tradesmen, neighbors, lawyers, agency people; pretty much the same people every year. There were three generations consisting of little kids running around and screaming, teenagers being cool, and the adults. Four generations if you counted Mike. A journalist, Craig had been embedded with the British army in Iraq, and Loomis thought the Saddam throw rug he'd brought back was "interesting." Interesting was in the process of replacing awesome where he came from. A neighbor, a French doctor, struck up a conversation with him. When the doctor asked about his impressions of France, Loomis said France was interesting. The doctor introduced him to his daughter Cindy, whose eyebrow and lower lip were pierced, and who was wearing black lace grunge gloves like Courtney Love's. Loomis was wearing earrings, tattoos, and an oversize cap on sideways. They were a twenty-first-century urban teenage couple from rock 'n' roll central. He slouched around her at first, while she pretended he wasn't there. Finally, exchanging words, they got up and walked off into the shadows around the corner of the terrace. It must have been half an hour later when one of the little kids came running all excited, shouting: "They're kissing, they're kissing." The teenagers had settled at a table in a cool dark place around the back, where they peacefully passed joints, until one thing led to another. (Later Loomis said it had been a French kiss, making it clear it wasn't his first.) After the bust by the little kids, grown-ups started snooping around. At eleven, the Eiffel Tower lights were turned on, and everybody rushed back to see them. The discreet table was suddenly in the front row. Embarrassed and stoned, not knowing what else to do, the two of them just sat there holding hands. Their body language recalled, despite all of the body art and piercings, suburban teenagers at a country club dance.

It would be nice to be able to say that the two of them lived happily ever after, but Loomis ended up with the worst of two worlds. He never followed up with Cindy because he wanted to be faithful to his girlfriend back in Tampa. He'd been talking to Jennifer by intercontinental telephone for hours every day. The time difference was cool—he could chill out, and call his chick at four in the morning, and it was still only ten where she was. The way it turned out, Jennifer broke up with him the day after he got home.

Before dropping out of high school, Loomis had learned how to operate a digital movie camera in his communications class. When he mentioned that he might like to be a filmmaker one day, Mike suggested a good way to start would be to write a pitch for a screenplay for a movie about his trip to Paris. Loomis said it was an interesting idea.

After his nephew had gone, looking at Paris out of the corners of his eyes, it dawned on Mike that, as it was said that the best thing about John Kerry was that he was not George Bush, the best thing about France was that it was not America. It was not a lot to ask of a country, to be not America. It was also the best deal he was likely to get, after having spent so much time and effort ducking into off-seasons, margins, and the holes in Swiss cheese. Interesting. What it came down to was that he was a free man who was difficult to manipulate. What more could he ask for?